# Becoming the Dawn

Copyright © 2023 Jay W. Song

Cover and Typesetting: Islam Farid
Edited by Shelby Leigh

Hardcover ISBN: 979-8-9886872-0-7
Paperback ISBN: 979-8-9886872-1-4
Ebook ISBN: 979-8-9886872-2-1

All rights reserved. No part of this book may be used, reproduced, distributed, or transmitted in any manner whatsoever without written permission from the author except in the case of brief quotations embodied in critical articles and reviews.

This is a work of fiction. Names, characters, places, and incidents either are the product of the author's imagination or are used fictitiously and any resemblance to actual persons, living or dead, business establishments, events or locales is entirely coincidental.

# Becoming the Dawn

Jay W. Song

When the sun
fails to shine,
you must reach inside,
and pull the light
out of yourself.

## Contents

*Part 1*
**7 Twilight's Veil**

*Part 2*
**105 Dawn's Mantle**

230 About the Author

*To those who feel like brighter days will never come*

# Part 1
# Twilight's Veil

## I UNDERSTAND DARKNESS

and the stars.
Hiding
shame,
wounds,
and scars.

I understand staring up at the moon,
howling like a wolf,
with the agony of faraway dreams
until, voice hoarse, I swoon.

I understand disappointment—
rose-colored glasses that shatter
and leave me seeing jaded green.

I understand shooting for the moon
and landing not among the stars,
nor even in the sky,
but in the dirt
with skinned, bruised knees.

I understand promises made
and broken as easily as bread.

I understand unrequited love,
and thinking you've found The One
only to realize later
that what you really found
was regret.

My name is Twilight,
and what I do not understand
is the Dawn.

I do not comprehend light
and the dew.
Exposing
dignity,
balms,
making all things new.

I do not understand gazing up at the sun,
smiling with a radiant face
that has seen its dreams come true,
that has found its Beloved One.

I do not understand love that holds the world up
in the palms of its hands,
bearing the weight of Atlas with effortless ease,
fountain never running dry, like an overflowing cup.

I do not understand lying face first in the mud
and finding the strength,
the humility,
to push yourself back onto your feet.

I do not understand hurt forgiven
and relationships made whole again
like an uncut loaf of bread.

I am the Twilight,
but I wish I was the Dawn.

## What do I do

when life is meaningless
and death seems like
a greater comfort?

What do I do
when the sun shines
on everyone
except me?

What do I do
when I doubt everything
I have believed, everything
I want to believe?

What do I do
when I feel left and forsaken?

What do I do
when I am tired
of hearing the same answers
that have never satisfied me,
and never will?

What do I do
when everything under the sun
is a mirage I see through?
When I can no longer pretend
everything is real?

What do I do
when soft clouds in the sky
seem to be an empty promise
for another life,
another day,
a future happiness
that will not help me now?

Jay W. Song

## A WOMAN KNELT.

It was a long time coming.

She was hemorrhaging hiddenly,
ravaged on the inside.

Her heart
was death
still beating.

Darkness cast a shadow
over her otherwise beautiful face.

The fountain of blood that erupts within—
you know not where,
you know not why.
The doctors who tried and failed to treat,
then ceased to try.
Pain so unimaginable you wonder
if you are just imagining.
The calendar sheets that slide down the wall
like sand in an hourglass—
each month ripped off,
tearing off a piece of heart and hope.
The nightmares of dying

become dreams,
dreams turn to daydreams,
daydreams to desire,
and desire to intent.
Now desire has led
to the precipice of action.

She realized how costly
it is to be healed.
It takes courage,
patience,
humility,
hope,
trust,
strength,
vulnerability,
honesty,
time,
will.

She decided then
it would be easier
to die.

One day, three days later,
she was sitting
in a field of lavender.

Her eyes watered the flowers,
and she thought about
how beautiful it would be
to die here.
*There is no better grave*,
she kept thinking.
*I could take a branch
and drive it through my heart
and end the dark.*

"That won't end the darkness,"
a voice said behind her.

Perhaps, somewhere deep inside,
she already knew that.

All she truly sought
in contemplating death
was an answer.

If not this,
then what could truly
end the dark?

## The Baobab Tree

*He failed me.* A young girl bolted out of her home, the screen door banging shut behind her. *He failed me.* She gripped the fraying rope tighter in her hand as she ran down the hills away from her house, eyes frantically scanning the tan grasslands for one tree, just one tree. *He failed me.* The air ripped savagely through her lungs like a chainsaw chewing through thick wood. She wheezed and began to cough so hard she doubled over and tripped, tumbling down the hill. Dead grass scratched her and caught in her hair, dirt flew in her eyes and mouth, and she landed face first on the ground when she finally reached the bottom. She struggled to lift herself back up. Above her she saw an enormous baobab tree, standing erect, silent, and imposing. Its branches did not sway at all, despite the cool, breezy wind at sunset. Most people would have thought it was a beautiful tree. All that concerned her was that it might be too tall to suit her purposes. Where was the rope, anyway?

She must have dropped it when she fell. *Ah—there.* She spotted it among the roots of the tree. As she reached out to grab it, one of the roots above ground suddenly branched off and grew over the rope. When she tried to pull on the rope, it would not budge. It was pinned beneath the root. The young girl got down on her hands and knees and tried to dig up the ground around the root. Her nails had all broken off down to the nub and she had almost grasped the rope when the root curled around it like a corkscrew, like a clenched hand that would not let go.

"I don't have time for this!" the girl shouted, pounding her fists against the root. They got bruises and splintered and bloody, but neither the root nor the rope would budge. "Just give me the rope, you stupid tree!"

"I cannot."

She looked up in surprise. The tree had not shifted in the slightest, the wind had stilled, and yet…and yet, she had heard a voice. Like a baritone or a drum, it was more felt than heard. She knew without a doubt someone was communicating with her, but there was absolutely no one out there save her and the tree.

"Why can't you?" she said timidly, quietly, almost afraid of another reply.

"Do you know what rope is for?"

"For tying up loose ends that don't belong," she gritted out.

"Sailors use rope to anchor their boats to the docks, so they are not swept away. Rescuers use rope to hold on to the one they are trying to save. Mountaineers use rope to secure themselves so that they are caught and held in their fall. Knots are strong, sturdy, and stable to guard something very precious.

"The purpose of a rope is to protect. What you are about to use that rope for is not right. What you came here, seeking to use me for, is not right."

The girl stood up, turned her back, and began to walk away from the tree. "Fine. I'll use something else then."

"I could stop you. I could save you. I could detain you against your will. But I will not. As I stated, a rope is meant to protect—not to ensnare—and neither is my purpose to ensnare. If you wish to go, then I must let you go—" The tree, the voice, whoever it was, sounded sad beyond its years. "But I have seen so many perish. Oh, how I long to take them into my arms and save them. That—that is what I am for! Yet I cannot. I will not misuse my power, no matter how many humans abuse the power and purpose of all that is."

The sadness, the ringing clarity of unrestrained sadness—it was just enough to move her to turn and take one last look at the tree. "How could you possibly save me?"

There was almost something of a glittering smile, a note of hope, in the voice. "How could a simple strand of twine possibly keep a boat anchored in the worst of storms? Or a thrashing, drowning man tethered to his rescuer? Or the weight of an entire human frame poised delicately between the mountainous peaks above and the rocky chasm below?"

For a beat, there was silence. Then...

"Come and see."

She could almost feel the roots beneath her feet quiver in anticipation of the weight of her choice. For the first time, it dawned on her that her life really was her own. She was free to shape the course of her life by her choices—forever. She was like the mountaineer, held only by a rope between the mountaintop above and the abyss below, and it was her decision and responsibility, hers alone, whether she let go of the rope and plummeted to her demise or whether she grasped it tighter and climbed upward toward the mystery of the view that awaited her at the top.

She looked hard at that tree and thought even harder. "What will become of me?" she asked. She wanted to know both how far she would fall and how high she would climb. She wanted to see both the depths and the heights at once, before she made her choice.

"My dearest, that is entirely up to you."

But such vision was not given to mankind.

"There is one more thing you ought to know about ropes," the tree began, when she had been silent for a long while. "They fray.

"They do not hold forever.

"And when they snap, you will fall, whether you chose it or not. At that point, climbing will no longer be an option."

These words alarmed the girl. "Will I really get to that point? Is there truly a point of no return?"

The tree sighed, sounding very tired again. "Yes. There are many, many individual threads that make up a rope—so too are there many, many chances for a human to change the course of their life. But one by one those threads come apart, until there is but one left. There comes a time in the life of every human when they are down to their last thread, their last chance to change things. And no one truly knows when their life has unraveled to that last thread, for who can say?

"I cannot say that this is not your last thread, dearest, yet neither can I say that it is. This is why delaying a choice could spell an unhappy end for any one of us.

"I have lived for 1,500 years—but if you delay this decision even until the morrow, who is to say I will still be here to save you then?"

The girl looked at the rope tangled among the roots of the baobab tree. The sun on its way down struck the tree just so, its slanting rays extending over the massive tree like reflections from eternity. In the dying, golden light—that sunlight most luminescent and alive even as it was most quickly fading into deepest darkness—the baobab tree took on a majestic quality. And the rope—it looked ragged, worn, and all the more horrendous when seen in that same light.

As she took a step forward toward the tree, the thoughts that had been running through her mind on the way down returned. *He failed me. Who's to say this "savior" won't, too?*

Yet, she suddenly found that hard to believe, looking at this tree in the molten sunlight. It was funny, but in the splendor of the oranges, yellows, and reds, it almost looked like a king. Not one like Henry VIII, but a good king, like the medieval fairytales parents told their children, like King Arthur and his knights—one who would fight for his people instead of grind them under his feet. And she remembered what that voice had called her—dearest.

She took another step forward, and another, until she was standing before the trunk of the tree. She put out the palm of her hand and touched it. It was solid, firm, strong, unmovable. She could not say why, but she found comfort in that.

"Alright. I will let you save me."

"Thank you, dearest," its voice rustled quietly, like a breeze. "It will be my joy and my honor."

Suddenly, two thick branches lowered themselves from their loft high in the sky until they were clasped together on the ground in front of her feet, the way people lock hands together to make a step stool.

"Come aboard the tree that will carry you safely home."

The girl stepped up onto the branches and held on for dear life as they raised themselves, and her along with them, back up into the starry sky. They stopped at a clearing—a flat, circular grove at the top of the tree covered from sight below by the canopy of its leaves. The floor was carpeted with leaves and, amazingly, flowers. A cardinal snoozed in a branch that stretched high above her head. Starlight sprinkled through the gaps in the tree leaves and branches. It was a veritable oasis in the desert.

She stepped off the branches that had been her elevator and wandered around the clearing. Whimsy moved her to pick a purple pansy and weave it through her hair.

"It's very lovely up here," she called to the tree, "but how are you going to save me?" The girl lay down in the flowers, her hair splashing out around her, and looked up at the night sky. "Even if you save me from suicide, I'll still die one day. So how is it that I can be saved?"

The flowers and branches swayed around her, as though the tree was laughing. "You are keen, dearest."

Suddenly, the wind stilled and all became ponderously silent.

"Little one, do you believe in the existence of the soul?"

The girl wanted to snort, but she dared not shatter the sacred silence. She merely shook her head.

"Do you believe in anything that perdures?"

This time, she did laugh, derisively. "My dad, who said he loved me, walked out on us, so you tell me. I'm going to die. You're going to die. The sun and stars will burn out and everything, even the best and most beautiful things, will die. So you tell me."

"Everything that you have said is true," the tree responded grimly. "Death is the end of all things, and yet. . ."

The girl slid forward on her stomach, peering over the edge of the clearing down at the tree. "Yet what?"

"That is the mystery of the soul."

She sighed, raising herself to her feet. "This was a mistake. As much as you want me to live, it just doesn't make sense. Even you can't make it make sense. Why does it matter whether I die today or fifty years from now, by a rope or by a stroke? It doesn't. It doesn't matter. And if you're trying to convince me with some life-after-death argument that killing myself is pointless, then I'll just kill myself in the afterlife too, and the life after that, and after that—as many times as it takes until I stay dead.

"So thanks for trying, but goodbye."

As she was about to step onto the elevator of branches, the tree stopped her and said, "Grant me one last question before you go."

She stood there in silence, anger roiling in her heart.

"Please, dearest."

Sighing loudly, she muttered, "Fine."

"Why is it...

"That you wish to die?"

"Because nothing matters!" she shouted, hot tears erupting from her eyes. "If pain is unavoidable, and I'm going to die anyway, why shouldn't I save myself fifty years of suffering? There's nothing more logical."

A long time passed before the tree said anything. When it finally did, it sounded older than time itself.

"I know you will not listen to anything I have to say. Therefore, take this."

The girl looked on in horror as the tree used two thick branches to pierce and pull back the bark at its base. Deep inside, there was an unbloomed red rose that had just barely begun to bud. He pulled it out of himself with a groan and handed it up to her. She stared at it, lying in the cradle of the branches as he waited for her to take it. So many thorns covered the stem that she could not touch it at all without being scratched.

Seeing how insistent he was upon her accepting the rose, at last she took it, holding it in the palms of her two hands.

"This," he panted, "is my heart. Now that it is exposed to the world, it will not last another 1,500 years. It will not last even 15 days."

She stared at the remarkably intimate gift he had given her—her, who had been nothing but cold to him. "Without this," she whispered, "won't you die?"

"Yes. When it is fully bloomed, then I will die."

"Then take it back!" she shouted, trying to place it back on the tree branch, but the branches lowered themselves back to his side.

"I cannot."

Nearly hysterical, she shot back, "Why?"

"A heart is a gift that cannot be returned."

The girl frantically paced around the grove, staring wide-eyed down at the rose in her hand. "You could have given this to anyone. You could have kept it for yourself and lived centuries, maybe even millennia, longer."

She stopped in the center of the clearing, tears streaming down her cheeks. "So why'd you give it to me?"

His voice was heartbreakingly tender. "Because," he murmured, "you are the one who said yes. Because you, dearest, are the one who let me save you."

Her heart began to swell, to feel as if it were bursting. Her eyes squeezed shut to try to keep back the torrent of tears, and she clenched her hands around the stem of the rose so hard it drew forth blood.

"You picked a lousy woman to give your heart to," she muttered, sniffling.

The tree rumbled and shook with laughter. "The heart wants what the heart wants."

She looked down at this rose, this vulnerable rose that was the tree's whole vitality. Gasping and catching her breath, she put her hand over her thumping heart.

"I..." she began.

"I am going to find a way to save your heart," she stated.

"No, dearest," the wind murmured close in her ear, "I am going to find a way to save yours."

She shook her head, trying not to smile at his nearness. "But I can't let you die!"

"Nor I you."

Trying to get him to change his mind was like arguing with, well...a tree.

"If I promise never again to try to kill myself, will you take your heart back?"

The tree replied gently, but sternly, "I told you, dearest, a heart is a gift that cannot be returned. I have given over my heart to you. It is totally yours now, and so am I. Do with it and me whatever you will."

She sighed. "You really did pick the wrong person," she said quietly.

"The wonderful thing about gifts is that they do not have to be deserved." The tree said simply.

"I think I need to go."

He did not stop her. He lifted his arms and lowered her gently back down to the ground. She stood there looking at him, the baobab tree with the gaping hole in its chest. She moved closer, reaching out to put the rose back in his chest, but a branch caught her wrist.

"I will not accept that heart back."

She smiled sadly at him. "You know I had to try."

She stood there looking at him for another moment, and then said, "What if I became your heart? What if I stayed inside you and kept you alive?"

The tree sounded almost amused now. "No, dearest, you were made to be free."

This was really it then. And yet... she could not believe it.

"I'll find a way," she insisted. "I'll come back for you."

The tree simply closed its eyes to sleep.

The girl ran back up the hill to her house, rope forgotten under the roots of the tree, now cradling a precious package in her arms. *I won't fail him*, she kept thinking to herself as her feet hit the ground. As soon as she got home, she ran some water and put the rose into a vase. She knew she had very little time to save his heart; roses were the very symbol of ephemerality and fragility. She could not freeze it into stasis like one could food—that would simply kill it faster. She could not deprive it of sunlight in hopes of arresting its growth—it would simply wither and die before it bloomed. Days passed, and without realizing, she spent more and more time thinking of how to save his heart than of how to kill her own. In fact, she ceased to think about herself altogether. All she knew was the one she was slowly coming to love.

In the end, she decided the best way to preserve the flower was to simply take care of it the best she could. She would sit out in the sun with the rose in her arms, clean its vase and replace its water daily, and with her determined love it began to unfold. It was beautiful, yet heart-wrenching. How, oh how, could he die at the height of life? He would die when it was fully bloomed, he said—not when it withered.

Late one night, when she was lying awake and restless in bed, staring at the rose on the nightstand, she realized it was almost bloomed. *I can waste what little time I have left trying to change what I cannot, or I can go and spend it with him,* she thought. Not a moment later, she was up and scooping the rose in her arms, never mind the thorns. It was the 14th night, and he had said himself the rose surely would not live 15 days. She ran out of the house, down the hill, desperately trying to make it to him before the night was over.

When she reached the baobab tree, his eyes were closed, and, thinking he was sleeping, she put her hand on the trunk and called to him.

There was no reply. All was utterly still.

Looking down at the flower in the light of the moon, she realized the rose had fully bloomed.

"Please don't be dead!" she cried, pounding on the tree. The wood returned a hollow, empty sound.

The girl slid down to her knees, the rose falling into the dirt as her hands went up to cover the sobs coming from her mouth.

"Why did you have to give me your stupid heart in the first place?" she screamed into the dark. "I knew it! I knew it from the start, how awful love is."

Staring numbly down at the rose, she remembered something he had said. *Do you believe anything perdures? Death is the end of all things, and yet...*

He had never answered her when she asked what that meant. Now she would never know.

The thorns hurt her again this time, more than ever, when she picked up the rose. *Totally yours.* She wanted to die, and yet she did not want to leave his heart alone. Not until it withered and followed him into death—then, *then* she would follow him, too.

The girl trudged up the hill to her house and ripped the rose from its vase. She stuck it in the freezer, hoping it would die faster.

The next morning, she opened the freezer door and found that the rose was perfectly pristine—as if it had not been dropped in the dirt and jammed in a freezer packed with ice cream and frozen meals. Alright, then. She could play that game. If she could kill herself, surely she could kill a single rose. She stuffed the rose in her dresser drawer, depriving it of all light.

The next morning, she opened the drawer and again, the rose had remained deepest red at the height of its bloom. She lit a fire in the fireplace, though it was late spring, and threw the rose into the flames.

On her way to her room, she turned back and stared at the burning rose for a moment. *Totally yours.* There was a stab of pain in her heart before she buried it under walls of stone.

The next morning, she tiptoed into the living room and peeked into the fireplace. All she saw was black and ashes. Grabbing a fire poker, she sifted around in the soot and gasped when she noticed a flash of red.

On her hands and knees, she combed through the ashes to find the rose. When she wiped off all the dirt, the rose still looked as it had three days ago.

*How is that possible? I saw it burn!*

She left the rose on the kitchen counter and tried to read a book to distract herself, but like insistent thorns, the rose kept pricking her heart. Finally, she could stand it no longer, so she grabbed the rose and went down the hill.

Even more astonishing than the rose that had burned but not been consumed was what she saw at the base of the hill. The baobab tree had disappeared. Roots, trunk, branches, leaves—simply gone, as though it had never been there at all. In the space where it once stood there was a field of fully bloomed roses stretching as far and as wide as she could see.

Roses. In the savanna, in the desert wilderness. How?

She stepped forth in bewilderment, clutching his rose—her rose—to her chest. Far off in the field she could have sworn she saw the figure of a person. But how, in the middle of nowhere?

She delicately stepped through all the roses, though they did not seem disturbed in the slightest by her footsteps, until she reached the figure. It was a man—tall, sturdy and strong, like—

Could it be him?

Impossible.

He turned around and seeing her, smiled.

"Are you—" she began.

"Is it really—" she tried again.

"Do you know me?"

He looked at her with eyes as warm as the earth on a summer day.

"Death ends all things, and yet..."

Niagara Falls must have gotten its name from the tears in her eyes as she realized what this rose had been trying to tell her the past three days, what he had been trying to tell her all along.

"It's you," she laughed. "It's really you, the baobab tree."

Suddenly, she felt ashamed as she looked down at the rose in her hands, thinking of how she had abused and wounded it.

The roses in the field rustled as he moved toward her, cupping his hand around her cheek and lifting her face up to meet his eyes.

"Death ends all things, and yet they can be restored to eternal life. I suffered death for you, dearest. Nothing more can harm me now. As you saw, that rose will never wither."

He rubbed her cheek with his thumb, gazing down at her with nothing but love. "As for all that you put my heart through, a heart is a gift that cannot be returned. No matter what you do, my heart and I are totally yours."

Her heart swelled with love at his words. She, who had sworn off love in the aftershock of her father, was falling headlong into it by the minute.

"I was going to kill myself when this rose died, you know," she said soberly.

"I know. That is why I gave it to you. Because it will never die."

Her eyes widened. "You mean you knew the whole time?"

He smiled sagely.

*How lovely love is,* she thought, beaming from ear to ear.

"I have something I want to give you," the girl said suddenly.

"A heart is a gift—"

"That cannot be returned, I know," she laughed. Reaching into her own chest, she said as she pulled forth a pink rose, "That is why I want to give you this. Since you can't return my heart either, you're stuck with me," she giggled.

He held out his palms as she placed the pink rose, covered in thorns, in his hands.

As she reveled in how deeply entwined their existences had become, she said peacefully, "I see now that if anything can fend off despair and give our lives meaning, it is our friendships and our loves. It is the sharing of our lives and hearts with others."

## Ultimatum of a stone heart

People figured out you could use stones
to build bridges, homes, shelters.
I found out you could use them
to build walls.

People mined in caverns for diamonds,
ravenous for their beauty.
I sought them
for their impenetrability.

I made this unbreakable rampart,
a tower of stone,
of steel,
of sheer determination of will.

But I am not just an architect.
I am an artist.
This wall looks human,
as David's marble looks flesh.

I encased my very self in statue,
wrapped in stone
like linen for embalming.

I remade myself of stone

to replace fragile flesh
and breakable bone.

Keeping myself hidden,
keeping myself safe.

Like a tree or a piece of furniture,
a brooding sentinel,
I watched the world,
seeing all yet
seen by none.

When the rains came,
my untouchable stone laughed.
"Water, what can you do to me?
You erode mountains,
and sweep men to their death,
but I shall not be moved."

When the earthquakes came,
my impeccable stone smirked.
"Earth, what can you do to me?
Shall you swallow me up into the ground?
I need neither air nor light,
so devour me."

When the winds came,
my unflappable stone set its face against them.

"Gale, what can you do to me?
You sweep up buildings,
 but I am the weight of a planet.
It is I who shall pull you
 into my devouring gravity."

When the fire came,
 my sturdy stone closed its eyes.
"Fire, O, fire. What can you do to me?
You bring man light and life—
will you kindle me?
There is no wood in me.
I am perfect.
Let the world burn."

Yet, safe within my stone tower,
I could not help feeling a certain emptiness.
When the outside world struck my wall,
it rang hollow
even though a person lived
hidden inside it.
Or perhaps,
had I been within this stone bulwark
for so long
that I had ceased to be a person at all?

After the rains, the quakes, the winds, and the flames,
then came a Man.

"What can you do to me,"
my haughty stone said,
"Mere mortal?"

He replied,
"Upon your stone
moss grows—
have you not noticed?
Your diamond has blackened,
cracks ravage your stone,
and your artistry has lost all human likeness.
Have you not seen these things?

Your apathy consumes like a rot.
Your complexity is that of Frankenstein's monster—
desecrated parts stuck together
in an unholy semblance of life.

Behold true humanity,
which is a complexity but a unity,
a peace not apathy,
a tranquility born from stillness yet not stagnation,
like unto stone in its strength.
Hardness of bone
balanced by tenderness of flesh.

Power of sinew
and grace of dove
crafted by hands
with intimacy and love."

My immaculate stone wall began to shudder.
Be still, oh heart I knew not could beat!

My threatened stone wall sneered
in the face of humanity.
"Have you only words?
Again I say,
what can you do to me, mortal?"

The Man approached me.
He said,
"I can come near.
Nearer to you than anyone else.

I can see.
My eyes are true.
Like the gaze of an archer,
two arrows shoot home
and always pierce the target.
I see through your opaque flesh
right down to your bone."

True to his word, he came nearer still.

Alarms rang in my heart,
and these feet,
which have not moved for decades,
twitched to life
and began backwards to step.

"O Tower, power does not gain access to your heart.
Fire would sooner burn itself out
than strike you with an ember.
Water would sooner die of thirst
than wet you with a drop of its spray.
Earthquakes would sooner rip apart the seams of this planet
than rend a crack in you.
Gale would sooner blow itself out of breath
than move a strand of your hair.
O stone heart, what indeed can touch you?
You have made yourself a perfect fortress, I fear.
You cannot exit,
and no one can enter to save you."

He stood mere feet in front of me now—
his feet swift as a gazelle,
while mine, trapped in crumbled stone,
were clumsy.

"Do you miss a glass of water?

A warm night by the fireplace?
The rolling thunder of the earth?
The breeze lifting playfully your hair?
Do you miss all these human things?
Do you wish to feel them again?"

"Do you wish to be vulnerable again?
Do you wish to feel beat again
a heart that exults and breaks?"

"Do you wish to feel again tears upon your cheeks,
fire in your heart,
grass beneath your wandering feet
and playful wind dancing with you?"

"Only you can choose
to trade solid and secure stone
for living flesh and musical bone."

My stone heart faltered,
but my flesh heart yearned.

Mortal man could do to me and my stone
what torrential rain,
shattering quakes,
blustery wind,
and devouring flames—
for all their power—could not.

Jay W. Song

Only another human could expose
the ultimatum of our existence.

To remain safe, hidden in stone,
or to reach for another with vulnerable flesh
and no longer be alone.

## If diamonds can be crushed,

then whose soul so firm cannot be?

I fear the shattering of my soul,
of all that I am,
every time I choose
to let new love
into my life.

For a heart can break in a thousand
different ways,
but there is only one way
to put it back together.

I fear
all those tiny,
little
pieces
will get lost
somewhere
in the breaking,
and without possession
of all the
shards of my heart,

I cannot return it
to the way it was.

What terrifies me most of all
is the fact that
one moment,
one person,
can change me
forever
and that afterward
I will never
be the same.

## If I lose my sparkle and shine,

if you find out I'm not real
silver
because I've turned your finger green—

If I'm iron instead of titanium,
if I rust and flake and peel,
and you worry I'll give you tetanus—

If someone brings me to you in a vase
with water and directions and feed packets and
thorns,
if you see that you have to take care of me
and I won't live forever like those
artificial
plastic
roses—

If I don't sleep through the night
without crying out,
if I sob myself to sleep sometimes—

If I catch a cold because I was out
playing in the snow without a coat—

Jay W. Song

If I fail to do what I really want
because I fear failure—

If you find me in a box abandoned on the street
and the box says "lost porcupine"
instead of "lost puppy"—

If I have a cold shoulder,
and a hot temper,
and a hard heart—

If I need you to remind me that I'm beautiful
and wipe away my tears on bad days—

If I need you to hold me
to keep me safe from myself—

If I break your heart in my heart break,
by asking if you really do love me—

If I sound like a car horn
when I laugh—

If I'm too clingy,
and get on your nerves,
and come looking for you in the middle of the night
because the bed is empty,
and you just went to get a glass of water—

If I'm afraid you'll love someone more than me
because I'm terrified of my best not being enough—

If I'm not perfect,
if I'm the me no one else knows
and not the one everyone loves—

Will you still love me?

Jay W. Song

## I THOUGHT THAT

flower bouquets
and romantic gifts
were things that I wanted
out of a relationship.

But now that I have them,
I realize
they don't matter
if they don't come from
someone who loves you
and who you love in return.

## My dad has a crack in his car windshield,

a small little chink from a rock
that flew into it while he was driving.

The next time I got in his car
a few weeks later,
the tiny pinhole of a fracture
was now a spiderweb
crawling in tendrils across the glass.

As I sat there,
staring through his shattered window
that had once only held
one tiny wound,
I thought about
all the things I had been putting off
and decided to do them
that day.

Because of that broken windshield,
I decided to tell you
that I wasn't in love with you,
because I realized that waiting

wouldn't make telling you
any easier
on either of us.

## You deserve someone

who will
stay with you
out of more than just guilt.

I deserve someone
who doesn't
make me uncomfortable
for reasons I can't explain.

You deserve someone
who loves you
instead of
just trying to convince themselves
that they do.

I deserve someone
who doesn't make me question
whether I'm settling
or not
by being with them.

We are
not each other's someones.

There is a strange
sort of freedom
in finally admitting that.

## When I told you

I didn't have any
romantic interest
in you

You asked me
what I was looking for
in a man.

I politely
dodged the question
because I didn't want
to hand you
a laundry list of the things I wanted
so you could try to
become them,
become him.

Somewhere out there in the world
is someone
who is looking
for all that you are,
and if I let you
become all that I wanted
then you would cease to exist,

and the one looking to love
you for who you already are
wouldn't be able to find you.

So no,
I will not
tell you
what I am looking for
in a man.
Even though
it is cruel,
all I can say is
what I am looking for
is not you.

## When I like

the way I look
in the mirror,
I spend so little time there.

I smile at myself,
and keep walking.

But when I don't
like what I see,
I plant myself
in front of the glass,
keeping vigil
like an unmoving statue.

I interrogate the
girl in the mirror
like a professor
administering an oral exam.

"Why
is your hair so frizzy and unruly?
Why
are your flaws so noticeable?
Why

can't you be beautiful?
When
will you be the person
I want you to be?"

The girl in the mirror
never gives me an answer.

She only looks back at me
with a devastated expression
on her face
and asks me a question
of her own.
"Why
are you so cruel to me?"

## If I try to follow

after the kids my age
and enter the door
to their secret clubhouse,
they will slam the door
in my face.

If I smile and laugh
along with them
I will be reprimanded
and told I don't belong.

If I am silent and distant,
they will question, "What is wrong?"
But they don't
really care
about the answer.

They call me names:
childish, naïve,
daydreamer.

When names cease to
cause sufficient damage

in their eyes,
they turn to rocks instead.

They hurl both
rocks and words
at me.
"Put down your books,
and get your head out of the clouds."

"Children can be cruel,"
my mother tells me,
"and they don't always
change
when they become adults."

So I resign myself to stare
into the door of humanity
that I shall never learn to open.

## Fine in the Clouds

I don't know
that I'll ever stop living my life
with my head in the clouds.

The world beneath the sky
is such a scary place to live.

## Somber Skies

The storm clouds roll in, and my feelings pour out—
this world has no hope left in it.
It makes me want to thunder with the clouds,
but I know I won't be heard.

## Where Earth Meets Eternity

I want the thousand lives
I've dreamed of living.
I want something less
than fantasy
but more
than reality.

I don't just want love.
I want the stars
that shine
at the edge of the universe

On the horizon
where Earth meets eternity.

## Icarus

Heavy,
too heavy
for air.

The grey matter
of our morals
weighs us down.

Yet it
keeps us afloat
between the two planes.

But we
are greedy,
want to fly.

Want to
show ourselves
we are good,

That we
can return
to heaven.

We cannot

fly, cannot
go back.

We cannot
give up
our dreams.

So we
give up
ourselves.

We break
off pieces
of our souls

And hide
them between
the holes in words.

We scatter
the scraps of
our hearts in the wind.

Together they
fly up
with wax wings.

We watch
with hands over
the holes in our hearts.

We watch
their wax wings
beat like our hearts.

We cannot
leave this world,
but our creations can.

They
are our
children now.

Like us,
they are
greedy.

They want
to fly
above the sky.

They want
to leave
their creator behind.

## Becoming the Dawn

We watch
their wax wings
melt.

We watch
our flaming dreams
plummet

To the
grave
at our feet.

We open
the burnt creation and
look inside.

We retrieve
the charred remains
of our hearts.

We put
them in
our chest

And we
weep,
for we are all Icarus.

## In the Forest

I put out the ashes
with my tears
and scatter them on the winds
of unborn memories.

Life does not rise from the ashes.
It dies there.
A spark does not the flame ignite.
The dark yields not to morning light.

In the forest I bury
the vestiges of my dreams
in unmarked graves
and walk on their bones.

In the forest grief hangs in the air
like an immutable fog.
Depression glistens on the ground
like an eternal morning dew.

## I MADE THE MISTAKE

of putting my dreams
in your hands,
thinking you could
achieve them for me.

You took them
and put them
in a dark cupboard somewhere,
forgotten and locked away,
or misplaced
with the dust bunnies
underneath the living room couch
because you didn't care about them
like I did.

I searched every inch
of your house
looking for my dreams,
but I could not find them.

It was only after
you were totally gone
from my life
that I realized

where I needed to look for them.
It was only after
the aftermath
of you
that I realized—
what I gave you
was only a copy.
The original manuscript
of my dreams
is still where it has always been.

Safe and sound
inside of me.

## You tried to take

my writing,
my words,
my voice,
away from me.

You tried to take
who I was
and turn her into
the woman
you wanted her
to be,
living the life
you wanted her
to live
so that you
could feel better
about yourself.

Everything I wrote
during that time
was scarred by you.
I do not recognize it
because with you in my life
I did not recognize myself.

## Jay W. Song

I do not know her
or her words,
and more than any
gaslighting,
manipulating, and
disregarding of boundaries
that you inflicted upon me,
that—
she—
was the scariest of all.

That you could have violated
my sacred, innermost heart
so deeply
that I no longer could see
myself in me
or in my words.

But I am taking myself back
from you,
rewriting everything I wrote
as that unrecognized stranger.
Taking back one word at a time—
my writing,
my words,
my voice,
myself.

## Sometimes,

things feel like
they're going well.

Sometimes,
you feel happy
and hopeful
and like maybe,
you're finally starting
to find your place in the world.

Then,
sometimes,
you go to the grocery store
and you get out of your car
with your handicap placard
hanging clearly
in the window
and a man
in a car
with confederate flag stickers
plastered to it
rolls down his window
and says,

"You don't belong here."

Jay W. Song

## When I walked outside

as a kid during the summer,
my biggest fear
was being stung
by a bee or wasp.

When I walk outside
as an adult,
my biggest fear
is being shot.

## I, Too

I, too,
have nightmares
and desire an embrace
to carry me through them.

I, too,
roll out of bed
just as you do
with bleary eyes and messy head.

I, too,
sit civilized
at the table
and eat with spoon and fork.

I, too,
dress myself—
first one leg,
then the other.

I, too,
have a job,
and maybe it is even I
who sits beside you.

I, too,
stare outside
the window
and daydream of
having a happy life.

I, too,
cry water
from my eyes
when my life wades through sorrow.

I, too,
have screamed
and thrown fits
when moved by the spirit of anger.

I, too,
pound my fists
upon the innocent earth
when I am taken by despair.

I, too,
feel
the presence of all these things,
and yet we are forbidden to share in them together.

I, too,
bleed

my red existence
when I am wounded.

I, too,
have a soul,
a loving God,
and a heartfelt religion.

I, too,
bare that soul
to all the world
and recoil when it is rejected.

I, too,
have sins
that I wish
to purge from all existence.

I, too,
have ancestors
whose actions and slights
I should not have to carry, but do.

I, too,
share in
the commonalities
and sufferings of existence.

I am

different in some ways,
it is true,
but does that make me
less than
you?

If my skin is darker than yours,
then does that entitle you
to be treated better
than me?

For a long time,
I thought the answer
to that question
was yes.

I accepted
the way
the world worked
and pretended
it didn't bother me.

But now
I am becoming
brave enough
to say

That I, too,
deserve
to be treated
just the same
as you.

## Who knew

that one little pain
could change
my whole world?

Just a little
sharp pain
in my hip
that appeared
out of nowhere
one day.

That little pain
was followed
by rashes
on my face
shaped like
butterflies,
chest pain
that felt like
a heart attack,
ribs driven apart
by swords.
Clumps of hair

down the drain
and bald spots
I tried to cover
with sadness and shame.

That one little pain
brought many other pains
with it,
but none of them
had a name.

Rheumatologists,
nephrologists,
cardiologists,
kidney biopsies,
and second opinions.
Tubes and tubes
worth of blood
drawn for labs
that gave me
no answers.

Years like this
wondering
if something was wrong
with me,
people telling me

## Jay W. Song

it was
my fault,
that it was
in my head.

My life had become
one big question,
and I could not accept
that it did not
have an answer.

But then,
one day,
it did.

The questions—
miles long, and manifold.
The answer—
short, and one.

Lupus.

The answer received,
the questions began again—
miles long, and manifold

But full of gratitude
that there would be
one question, at least,
I would never have
to ask again—

"Is it all in my head?"

## "You're sick because

God's punishing you
for not giving your life to him."

At the time,
I believed you.
I listened to all the voices,
yours the loudest,
telling me
that my body falling apart
was my fault.

But now,
despite my
three chronic illnesses,
I can see
that the sick one
was not me.

## "You're fine," she said

after I told her
that sometimes
I experienced pain
so excruciating
I could not walk.

"You're fine," she said
after I told her
that I was
menstruating
every week
of the month,
after I told her
that the bleeding
would never stop,
after I told her
that my sheets and clothes
looked like
a crime scene.

"You're fine," she said,
so I went on my way

until I could no longer
get out of bed.

It took
so much
to disagree
with a doctor,
to say,
"I'm not fine."

But I kept saying
"I'm not fine,"
until I found someone
who believed me.

And now
I have two sets
of surgery scars
around my belly button
to prove it.

I wasn't fine,
but I am now
because I
advocated for myself,
because I would not
stop shouting
until someone listened.

I wasn't fine,
but I am now
because I realized
that a patient
in modern healthcare
does not get
to be
just a patient.

We must
learn to be
vigilant
warriors,
fighters,
self-advocates,
or else
we become
victims.

Jay W. Song

## As babies, most of us

enter this world
with crying and tears.

Yet, knowing this,
or perhaps despite it,
we still try to deny
that pain
is a part of life.

## Coming to Terms

My dear child,
I don't know
if I will ever meet you.

You don't exist
and yet
I have
so much love for you,
so many plans
for how I will raise you,
so many dreams
of how I will bring
love into your life.

I may never know your name.
It seems
more and more unlikely
that you will ever grow
and make a home
in my womb,
but you already have
a home in my heart.

I may never

be able
to hold you at my breast,
but even now I
hold you
in the heart
beating in my chest.

# The Spirit Duplicator

"I love you, honeybear." The sound of her husband's gentle, content chuckle rang in Eloise's ears, and she wished it would echo forever like a song on repeat. But cassette tapes wear out, and CDs get scratched, and MP3 players and iPods become obsolete, and phones get replaced year after year. A song can only be replayed so many times before even the way we listen to music itself changes. Eloise knew this, painfully, and knew, too, that one day the cassette tape of her husband's voice would deteriorate and no longer play her favorite sounds.

"Tell me again why you call me honeybear." Everything about Eloise, from her words to her smile that barely touched her teary eyes, was wrapped in a thick duvet of wistfulness, as if it would keep her insulated from the pain of loss.

The chill breeze of a cloudy autumn afternoon teased them, lifting up the edges of their red gingham picnic blanket and making them draw their jackets tighter around their shoulders to keep the cold from their necks. "You know why I call you honeybear." He tilted his head the way he always did when he was amused and exasperated with her. She took a photograph in her mind of the expression, but even photographs get damaged or lost or faded.

With his left pointer finger—the one that was scarred, she knew, from the time he sliced it open trying to make his mom breakfast in bed as a child—he indicated her thermos of peach tea, and her slice of key lime pie, and then her heart. "You are my honeybear because you love sweet things, and you are just as sweet as the food you eat."

The first time he had called her that, she blushed terribly and hid her face in embarrassment. Now, she simply smiled, preserving every word to memory as though her mind was an audio recorder. But even voice recordings become warped and garbled with static over time. Her husband was dying, and was there not anything she could do to preserve the traces of his existence forever? She was committing every moment to heart, to memory, for now, but what of that inevitable day when her mind failed and her memory faded into the horizon with the distance of time? Pictures, recordings, souvenirs and mementoes—these, too, one day would fail her and be lost. Was there not any technology that could keep the man she so loved alive until the day she, too, died and went to be with him?

"You are sad and sour, my honeybear," her husband murmured, catching her attention with his hand on her cheek.

"I am simply going to miss you. Very much," she sighed, staring up into the grey sky that would soon separate the two of them, one to go above and one to remain behind below.

He laughed as though she had just said the silliest thing or a horribly corny joke. "Honeybear, I am not gone yet."

"But I know that one day you will be and that thought colors your presence with sadness even now!"

With this, he could not argue. This was not their first discussion about Eloise's sorrow over his impending death, and yet, they never escalated into fights. He never argued. He simply held her in his arms, and they enjoyed that happy moment tinged with sadness as best they could.

After that day near the end of his life, Eloise's moments with her husband were no longer striated with sadness. Indeed, to an outside observer, one would think the two were in their newlywed phase of life, so ecstatic together were they. As if the autumn breeze had lifted all their cares upon its incorporeal back and bore them out to whatever faraway place the wind runs. The two spent October nights lying in the grass in their backyard, their sides stitched seamlessly together and fingers pointing out constellations and shooting stars like young star-crossed lovers. In the mornings they lounged in the bed, letting the sunlight pour over their skin like a liquid, golden salve, like sweet honey. Then, when the sun was high in the sky, came the pillow fights and the laughter and the pounding of footfalls upon the hardwood floor, and the house felt within its bones more life than it had within itself in years. Such happiness passed day after day, with not a trace of the sadness that had once enveloped all. The first red-orange leaves appeared, nestled deep within the foliage and barely visible, and then the trees began to turn inside out, exchanging their green outfits for red and orange and gold sweaters, then deciding to shed those outfits for the white gown of snow gifted by the sky. The trees, they bled and died, but he who was fated to die and she who was fated to mourn, did not. He walked on, and she smiled, without melancholy, without tears. She celebrated her luck, for her husband now was healthier than he had ever been in his life. Since that wonderful day when their luck turned around, there hung in the air, in the house, and about them both the unmistakable, saccharine scent of alcohols, but that, she could easily ignore, and with time, it faded.

With time, so did he. His skin became paper thin, brittle, and yellowed. His black hair, which she had always thought made him especially dashing, dulled like a deep black ink that had been exposed to the sun for too long. The clarity in his eyes disappeared. He was a book whose words had evaporated and whose pages were crumbling away. His entire existence became illegible.

When her husband's luck ran out this time, sadness did not return to Eloise. Instead of mourning that which was passing on, she clung to it, even more determined to save it. Yet, no, that was not quite it. Before, she wished to save his memory. However, in that first moment when her husband went from a dying man to a living one, something shifted in the both of them, and it was not their luck.

In the middle of the night, a few weeks after Christmas, Eloise threw back the sheets on her side of the bed and stepped into her slippers. A hand of frail fingers latched around her wrist as she stood to leave. The tighter he held her, the more flecks of dust crumbled off of him.

He was like a dehydrated husk, a dilapidated castle of sand falling to pieces in front of her.

"Where are you going?"

She smiled kindly at him, and while she could hide her thoughts, her body belied her, and the expression emerged as more of a grimace. "Don't worry, dear. I'll be right back. Just getting some water."

"Why do you call me dear?" The windows to his soul were wide open, but no soul could be seen inside. "Who are you?"

"I am your honeybear." Her voice shook. This was not the man she loved. Not any longer. He was dying again. But their luck would change, just like it did last time. He would recover and be himself again. She was sure of it.

"What is a honeybear? Who are you?"

She left him then, leaving a small pile of dust behind on the bed from where she'd had to pry his fingers off of her. Eloise walked down the stairs to the basement, a pall shadow over her face, and closed the door. Beneath the door and around the sides seeped the thick, sweet smell of alcohols.

By the next morning, fortune smiled on the couple again. Death was beat back from the warmth of their doorstep and consigned to the outer darkness. Her husband had recovered from his illness again. If once was a miracle, then what was twice? Fate? The universe rooting for them, cheering on a couple it could not bear to see torn apart? Eloise did not care, as long as he was still with her.

When she came up from the basement that morning, he sat on the edge of the bed waiting for her. His hair was not quite as saturated as it once had been, and his face, a hue paler. Death had crept closer.

"You're up early, honeybear," he said lightly, a boyish smile on his face.

As long as she was still his honeybear, all was right with the world.

She sat beside him on the bed, resting her back against his front and gazing up at him with love and relief in her eyes. "I thought we might go ice skating today. All the children should be back in school from Christmas break now, so we may be blessed to have the ice all to ourselves."

He leaned down and nestled his chin in the crook between her shoulder and neck. "That's a lovely idea. We could dance on the ice like the figure skaters you so enjoy watching at the Olympics."

When he spoke of the Olympics, tears slid down Eloise's face like droplets of rain on a window pane. The next Winter Olympics was two years away—would he get that many miracles to be able to see it with her? How many times could she keep doing—?

"Are you doing that terribly depressing thing where you miss me when I'm not even gone yet?" her husband chided, with a teasing tone in his voice.

"No." It sounded quite serious and irrevocably final, that one word. Certainly not playful and flirtatious, as his tone had been.

"Then why is my honeybear a weepybear?"

Eloise snorted. Even now, with the sadness and the death creeping back in much faster than she liked, he was an expert at making her laugh. "I just have a lot on my mind. Thinking of how I can save you."

"Look at me, Eloise."

And that, she knew, was his serious voice. The one he would have used when their children were in trouble, if they'd ever had the chance to have them. If it hadn't now been too late.

She lifted herself up from his chest and turned to face him, their knees touching.

He wrapped his hands around hers. "You cannot save me. You can only love me."

"But if I cannot save you, then how can I love you? How can I love that which is dying and leaving me at every moment?"

He lifted one hand and used it to gently massage her hair. "Have I, at this very moment, left you?"

She stayed silent.

"Then you can love me. You can love me as I am right in front of you, as I breathe."

Eloise stared at his eyes for a moment, and then, finding them more diluted than she remembered them, flicked her gaze away. "And when you are gone?"

"Still you can love me. By accepting your grief, instead of fighting against it. Accept the hole in your heart as a sign that there was once something wonderfully beautiful there, and be thankful for what was, knowing that for a thing to end is better than it to never have been at all, and bid it farewell, and then love me still, by living your life fully and intentionally, with joy. Love me by mourning for as long as you need, and then love me still, by allowing your mourning to end and yourself to be happy again.

"Love me by refusing to become bitter, my sweet honeybear."

Eloise did not feel like going ice skating after that.

The ensuing months were much the same as the period that had followed the first miracle, except the house and its inhabitants were not quite so exuberant and alive as they had been before. Eloise could no longer delude herself that he was cured, that a permanent solution had been found, that death had been driven away with finality. With the knowledge that she was simply delaying the inevitable, she became melancholy again, and as time passed, it, and he, only worsened. The first time he recovered, at the beginning of autumn in September, he had been well until almost the end of January. The second time he miraculously recovered, that day they had sat on the bed and talked about ice skating, he soon began to fall apart by the first hints of spring in mid-March.

She noticed it on their walk to look at the blooming dogwood trees. Walking hand in hand down the city sidewalks, she suddenly felt his warm, solid flesh turn to brittle paper, and the crumble of dust and sands against her palm. His movements became stiff and jerky, and he questioned who she was and where they were. With cold dread she hurried home, dragging him along behind her. She left him standing in the living room, while she raced down to the basement. Alcohol spirits, so strong they dizzied her, filled the room and seeped through the cracks, and soon, death was gone again, replaced by the familiarity of the one she loved.

The next time, in April, they were outside at the park, standing on a red bridge over a pond and throwing bread out to the ducks. She happened to look at his reflection in the water, and black ink seeped from his eyes, running down the paper of his skin like a handwritten book left out in the rain. The ducks forgotten, she rushed him home again, sprinting headlong into the basement. This time, the spirits were so strong they put her in bed with a migraine for two days straight. But her husband, healthy and whole again, was there to care for her, so it was all right.

Eloise never imagined a life like this. At every moment, trying to move on and enjoy it, while at the back of her mind, fearing that her loved one would fall apart again, forcing her to drop everything to prop him back up. How could Eloise have appreciated the beauty of the dogwoods, their petals drifting in the wind, when all she was thinking of was the fear of him drifting away? How could she have a relaxing afternoon lazing about the park and feeding the ducks, when she had to race home in the middle of it because her husband was melting from his eyes? And the cost of saving him was not just his rapidly deteriorating life, but now, too, her own.

Every month, it simply got worse. His "miracles" were not even lasting a full month now. In May, she had to race to the basement twice. In June, three times. By July, it was every week, and by August, every other day. Eloise became so ill she could no longer even enjoy her time with him. She would simply revive him and then lie in the bed, feeling as though she were dying.

One day in September, nearly a year from when all this had begun, she hobbled down to the basement, and when she was finished and knew she had a few good hours before he started to disintegrate, she put on sunglasses—for her eyes were weak—and grabbed her cane by the door—for she could not walk far—and she made her way to the thrift store downtown. She hoped the man who had sold her what she thought was a cure was still there. Only he could tell her why all of this was backfiring so horrifically. He promised her that she could have more time with her loved one, but this was not the kind of time she wanted. Not anymore.

There it was, a cheap little building, with the paint peeling, and the OPEN sign hanging crookedly in the window. She struggled to push the door open with her emaciated arms. When she finally made it inside, she saw him there, sitting behind the counter in an office chair, leaning precariously back in the seat with his feet propped on top of the register.

"You look familiar..." he said, trailing off as he spit the shell of a sunflower seed into a container. "Ahh, yes, you were that beautiful lady who came in here about a year ago and bought the spirit duplicator. Said your husband had just died the day before."

A year. A whole year of this heaven turned to hell of her husband being gone but not gone.

"The spirit duplicator—it's not working the way you said it would work. He keeps oozing ink, and his skin turns to paper and crumbles away, and he forgets who I am, and every month he fades faster and faster, to the point where I have to duplicate his soul a few times a day!"

The shopkeeper sat up straight in his chair and took his feet down from the register. "Oh, you poor darlin', don't you know what a spirit duplicator is?"

She shook her head, tears running down her chin from sheer overwhelm.

"It was the precursor of nowaday's copy machines, back in the 20th century. It makes a copy of the original using alcohol spirits, which I reckon is why you're lookin' so sick now. You've used it too much. Spirit duplicators can only make a limited number of copies. Each one of 'em will come out more faded than the last. I told you when you bought it that it would give you a little more time with your loved one."

Eloise banged her bony fists on the counter. "So there's nothing to be done for it? He's died once and now even his ghost will die, and I'll be left with nothing?"

The older man looked pitifully at her. "You'll have your memories, miss. Ya best make the most of the time ya have left, because there likely ain't many more copies left in that old machine. Tell 'im goodbye, for real and proper this time. It's probably the last chance you'll get."

She hunched over the counter, her head buried in her arms. "I don't want to say goodbye. I can't."

She felt him pat the top of her head, but it wasn't the same as when her husband did it. Nothing would be the same. Even this reality of him as a ghost to which she had grown accustomed—now even that would never be the same.

"He's gonna go, whether ya say goodbye or not. So ya might as well bid him farewell and thank him for the times ya did have together."

As Eloise struggled with the door on her way out again, she heard the shopkeeper say, "Even that spirit duplicator o' yours that can raise ghosts to life for a while can't keep 'em here forever. Not even all the technology humanity has made throughout its long history can keep a man from truly dyin'. Sad, ain't it?"

For the last time, on the anniversary of the day her husband died, Eloise went down to the basement. She thought of the last thing they had done while he was alive together, that picnic with the key lime pie and the peach tea whose flavors she could still taste in her mouth even now. For the final time, she placed her husband's ashes on the spirit duplicator and brought his spirit back to life.

He appeared by her side.

"Are you ready now, my honeybear?"

She stared down at the machine, angry, frustrated, disappointed. Tired. "Ready to say goodbye?"

He placed a strong, comforting hand on her shoulder. She felt as though that was the only thing holding her up. "No, dearest honeybear. Ready to love me instead of trying to save me."

With an audible sob that contained all the grief she had refused to allow herself to feel this past year, she threw herself into his arms. "I wish I had spent the time I had with you better."

He held one hand against her back and used the other to stroke her hair. "I don't wish that. I wouldn't change a moment of the time I had with you for anything. Even the arguments, the sadness, the distance. It was still time with you, and by virtue of that, it was perfect time. Every moment of my life that I spent with my honeybear was absolutely sweet."

She laughed, and cried, and clung tightly to him until she began to feel his skin turn to paper again.

"Thank you for the joy of being your wife. I will accept the sorrow of your passing as a sign of the utter happiness I had with you while you were living. Goodbye, my Pooh-bear."

He crumbled to what he was and had always been in her arms: ashes.

## These hands

can't sow seeds
in the past
or harvest fruit
from the future.

These hands
only have now.

These hands
only have this
patch of dirt,
this rusty shovel,
this dream
of a beautiful flower,
this memory
of all that grew here before.

These hands
have never worked
a field,
have only ever
dug through the sky
sifting for stars.

These hands
can't decide
whether to plant
a rose
or a poppy.

These hands
get tangled up
in the fear
of growing
imperfect things.

These hands freeze
even in the warmth
of late April
because they
expect the best.

These hands
get discouraged
with the truth—
that growing,
creating,
tending
life
takes many tries

and demands many mistakes
to be learned from.

These hands
can't tell a
root from a weed.

These hands
don't know
when a plant
needs water
or when it needs
to sit in the desert.

These hands
just ache
for something,
anything,
to make
grow.

But these hands
will settle
and these hands
will still,
waiting until
the earth
is ready to till.

## Winter—

Dead, cold, all around—
Everything cut off
From life.
Sorrow,
Who am I,
And what is life?
Why is life—
Why death?
Why my life and not my death?
Winter, cold, death,
Sorrow, meaninglessness, anger,
Choking—
Cut off—
Leaves in the wind,
Fragments cut off
From trees,
Trees deprived of fullness.
Loss, barrenness, emptiness
And then—

A greenhouse.

Climbing ivy,

Pink flowers bursting in the corner,

Jade plants unjaded by the death of everything around them.

Transparent glass so wonderful, sign of seeing and being seen.

*What would it feel like to walk inside?* she wonders.

But for her, for now, it is enough to see.

To see that there are pink flowers and promises of spring,

Even when all she can find in her own life are weeds.

She can't even draw, yet she wishes for a notebook and a pen, but

How to capture the hope with which those pink blooms fill her heart?

A messy poem with beauty breaking through—

Just like the greenhouse.

A short blip of light and beauty in the wasteland,

A reminder spring blossoms are on the way—

A greenhouse.

# Part 2
# Dawn's Mantle

## Magnolia

Every day
on my walk home from school,
I would pass a magnolia tree.

It stood all by itself
in the center of a clearing,
nestled off in the back corner
of the town park.
As if the world could not bear
its very grandiosity
and segregated it to the shadows.

Yet, the light still found it.
The sun echoed its rays
directly across the magnolia
at 3 o'clock every day,
the time I would be walking home.

I found something relatable
about this tree, and
something sad.
It was always green.
It never bloomed,
never blossomed,

never let the wind carry
its dreams far away
on the tail of the breeze.
It never died,
never shed
the burden of its past.
It simply stood there,
alone,
forgotten,
living yet not flowering,
living yet not wilting.

The more I walked past it,
day after day,
in summer,
winter,
spring,
and fall,
the more I became convinced.

This magnolia tree was stuck.
Just like me.

Like the magnolia,
I had been rooted here all my life.
Seen the same sights,
the same people,

every day.
While the world went on,
growing,
changing,
I was stuck—
fully matured,
and yet never bloomed.
A young woman,
still sleeping with a bear at night,
still mistaken for a child.
Still hearing the well-meant words
of surprise:
"You're too young—"
to be
to do
to have
whatever I am chasing after.
Still having never fallen in love.

Yes, as I walked back home
every day,
I would see that magnolia,
and wonder if either of us
would ever bloom,
would ever grow up.

One day,

the stagnant magnolia
rippled.

There was a man
standing beneath
the magnolia tree.

I took a detour
and ventured into the park,
making my way back
to the little clearing.
The man did not hear me,
so I took note of him
without him taking note
of me.

He wore a white
short-sleeved button-down
and crisp
denim jeans
stained with dirt
at the knees.
He must be the groundskeeper,
I realized.

"You must have seen plenty of magnolia trees,"
I said to him.
"Why stop and admire this one?"

He didn't take his eyes
off the tree,
but the corners of his mouth
curved.
"You must have seen plenty of sunsets,"
he replied,
"Why stop and watch another?"

I smiled a little,
taken aback
by his quiet wisdom.
A gardener with the voice
of a poet,
the mind of a philosopher—
how unusual.

His eyes moved
to look at me clearly,
and they were
green and brown
like the magnolia.

"Who are you?" I asked,
meaning his name,
but my heart
meant much more than that.

"What do you seek?"

he replied,
still looking deeply
at me.

"What do you mean?"

He opened his arms,
gesturing to all the world around us.
"What do you want
most of all?
What do you
dream of
lying awake at night?
What do you
wish for
on shooting stars
and birthday candles?
What do you strive for
without even noticing?
What desire
covers all your thoughts
like climbing ivy?
What do you
long for so much
it hurts?"

I put my hand over my heart,

listening in silence,
feeling it beat.

I didn't know.

Perhaps that
magnolia
had been stuck for so long
because it spent all its life
trying to be
something other than
a magnolia tree.

## Just because trains exist

does not mean you have to ride them.

Just because chicken feet exist
does not mean you have to try them.

Just because convents exist
does not mean you have to join them.

Just because someone asks you on a date
does not mean you have to go with them.

Just because you are dating someone
does not mean you have to stay with them.

The existence
or presence
of someone or something
within your life
does not impose an obligation
upon you.

You should only ride trains
if you enjoy train rides.

You should only try chicken feet
if you think you will like the taste.

You should only join convents
if you want to give your life to God.

You should only accept a date
if you are interested in the person offering.

You should only stay in a relationship
if you feel fulfilled and safe within it.

You should not make a habit
of doing things you don't want to do
for reasons or pressures
coming outside of you.

Doing this
will only make for
miserable train rides,
upset stomachs,
insincere nuns,
unhappy dates,
and unhealthy relationships.

The world
has enough people
doing things for the wrong reasons
already.

I am deciding
to no longer be one of them.

## Dear Human

I love the things
people hate
about you.

I love the way
your hair frizzes
in nervous sweats.

I love how your forehead
is the ideal spot
to place gentle kisses.

I love how your teeth,
crooked, poke through
your smiling lips.

I love how your cheeks
attract the soothing caress
of cupped hands.

I love your skin,
scarred with the words
of your story.

I love the hairs on your arm

that jump with you in fear
and curl in the rain.

I love your stomach
and its folds that roll
like hills and valleys.

I love the way your shoulders
offer comfort and repose
for weary heads.

I love your chubby feet—
the baby toes and the big one
that went to market.

I love your lungs
and their capacity for laughter
and tears.

I love your navel
and the ghost of the cord
that connects you to this life.

I love the lips
that turn red
when kissed.

Jay W. Song

I love the tongue
that swallows and savors
words and flavors.

I love the pimples
that protect you
from perfection.

I love the shades
of your people,
manifold in their colors.

I love the warmth
your hand
brings mine.

I love the way fingers slip
unnoticed into your mouth
when in deep thought.

I love your constant
war between
dark and light.

I love the lines
in your face that crinkle
like a well-loved book.

I love your eyes
that can be an open window to your soul,
or a closed door.

I love the way sadness
spills out of your heart
through your eyes.

I love the way joy
explodes from you
in snorts and giggles.

I love the way anger
seeps from a crack
in your soul.

I love the way guilt
chews through your heart
like worms in an apple.

I love how you
can carry your own soul
as well as another's.

I love how you
ignore the anchor of your sins
and build toward the heavens.

## Jay W. Song

I love the way
you clothe yourself in shame
after all these years.

I love how you
know when to hold on
and when to let go.

I love how you
were cast from paradise,
and so try to build your own.

I love how you love
with the passion of gods
and all your being.

I love how you hate
with the spite of demons
and all your sins.

I love how you forgive
slowly, but with
all your honesty.

I love the way
your flaws
define you.

I love the way
you fight against them
and who you are.

I love the moments
when you come to
accept them and yourself.

I love the way
you express yourself
in 7 billion unique ways.

I love the way
we are the same as each other
in all the ways that matter.

## The Wedding Band

It runs round and round.
It never ends.
Coming back to the beginning,
it runs to the end again,
and coming to the end,
it begins.
Never ceasing,
renewed every moment.

And could you break it,
even if you tried?
Could you take solid gold
and shatter it like glass,
or snap it like a twig?
Could you bend it like rubber,
or burn it with your anger?

Is it ever removed?
If the mountains fall
into the sea,
and the sky goes dark,
and the birds silent—
could the collapse of the universe

ever loosen it even a little,
or cause it to fall off?

It runs round and round.
It never ends.
A threefold cord
is not easily broken,
but a band
knit from the cords of love
shall outlast even the sun.
On that day when the last star goes dark
and the planets cease to move,
it runs round and round.
It never ends.

Is it like a magnet,
its attraction dulled by distance?
If you remove yours,
and cast it into the depths of the sea,
is that the end of mine and me?
If you grow wings
and fly to the furthest
reaches of the dawn,
if you harden your heart
and descend into the deepest
depths of hell,
has the magnet lost its spell?

## Jay W. Song

If you but look,
you will see,
like a comet it will tear through the sky
to follow you to the heights,
like a rock it will fall through the sea
to reach you in the depths of where you are,
like the wheel of a car ever turning,
it will not cease
until it has come to rest again
by your side.

Does it startle like a bird?
Could you,
with your tactless steps,
ever scare it away?
Is it fickle like the breeze,
caressing you one moment
and leaving you the next?
Is it like the magma of a volcano,
cooling and hardening
in the aridity of your lovelessness?
This, a bird?
You need not fear
scaring it away—
can anyone scare off
the lion from his pride?

More likely you will fear it,
as it asks you for all.
It is faithful as the ox
that helps the farmer pull the burden
every day.
It is like the core of the earth,
always molten,
never cooling
despite the years.

It runs round and round.
It never ends.
It is seamless,
without a hitch.
There is no bump or scratch,
dent or nick
which can hinder it
from running on.
Even if you
should take it off
and put it down
and hide it away in a drawer,
like a clock,
it runs on and on.
Yet unlike time,
it never runs to an end.

Unlike time,
it can go back.
It can undo
the wounds that have been done.
Unlike time,
you can begin again
from where you left off.
You can put it back on
at any moment
and find that it
has waited for you.
It runs round and round.
It never ends.

As the wedding band goes,
so does my love.
From eternity to eternity,
round and round,
my love chases after you.

## How Love

How love?
How indeed.
Having been trampled
by those I thought I loved,
or those who claimed to love me,
I ask,

How love
once again
in the face of these?

How love?
How cruel.
Breaking human hearts,
I refuse the pain of it.
For this heart, duel.
I will defend its safety to my death,
its solitude to my last breath.

How love?
How enduring.
Cliff side against the waves,
faithful rock,
lost, drowned souls securing.

JAY W. SONG

How love?
How unveiling.
A piercing rapier
strikes me, thus revealing.

How love?
How healing.
Seeing all the wounds
and faults
residing within me,
yet still loving
just the same.

How love?
How freeing
to begin with loving
myself again
after being shattered
by the love of other humans.

## Not this house.

I hate this house.
How could this be the place you want me to live?
Where I spend all my days?
How could this be what you want for me?

I hate this house.
Please, give me a new one.
It is so far away from the city,
away from the bustle,
the people,
the entertainment.

It is too small for me to spread my wings—
not my style,
not modern enough,
no cozy amenities, just the basics.

I would be ashamed to bring friends here.
The roof leaks in the back corner of the kitchen
when it rains.
The land is so big I spend all day mowing the grass.
You can hear animals at night,
coyotes howling,
raccoons rustling through my trash.

Why did you give me this house—
when you gave all my friends much better houses?
Bigger ones,
with jacuzzi tubs,
open concept kitchens with giant islands for a family to gather round,
a room for each kid so no one has to share,
a basement for the husband,
a bonus room for the wife,
so everyone can have their own space,
time to themselves.
A two-car garage,
and close to the city,
so they never have far to drive for work or groceries.

Yet here am I, with the scraps of the table—
a passed over, forgotten thing,
left with all the suffering in the world
that no one else wants.
I hate this house,
and I almost hate you.

In time, you will discover
all that I want you to see
about this house,
and about me.

I scoff at you.
There is nothing
that can unmake this pain in my heart,
no matter what you say or do,
no matter how much time shall pass.
For to find good in evil
is to excuse evil,
and to find happiness in sorrow,
is to invalidate your sorrow.
I refuse it.

\*\*\*\*\*

The roof still leaks when it rains and overflows
the bounds of my patience.
I am still mad at you, and find you
difficult to love.
But,
today I discovered wild vines of blackberries,
dark as a countryside night away from city lights,
lush as morning dew that makes yesterday's old grass fresh and new.
I picked them and brought them inside,
and they were delicious.

\*\*\*\*\*

I had such dreams—such grand, wonderful dreams—
and yet
if not even the smallest things in life
go according to plan,
then how can I expect anything
to live up to these beautiful dreams?
The air conditioning broke for the third time
this summer—
my closest thing to a jacuzzi tub the pool of my
own sweat.
From the stagnant air I fled, seeking breezes light and
sweet
and a surprisingly lovely sight did I chance to meet.
A flock of bluebirds startled by my presence
exploded from their tree in an azure storm
to take wing in the sky with featherlight reverence.

*****

It's not about the house, you know.
Yes, I know.

*****

In the solitude of this place,
the pain of my heart speaks
loudly, clearly,

and I am forced to confront it.
Terrible memories rise to the surface,
plain to see as leaves floating
atop a still pond.
Wishing I could forget them,
I scoop up the leaves in my hand
and hold them out for the breeze
to carry away.
But there is no breeze here.
All is still.
There is no distraction in this house.
Only you
and my gnarled, confused existence.
It is too raw, honest.
Neither sugar-coated like my dreams,
nor jaded, like my reality.
Both relentless and gentle,
it simply is.
Just as you are.
That is why I hate this house.
It reminds me too much of you,
whom I have given up on.
But perhaps I could try
to love you again.

*****

JAY W. SONG

In the city
of my youth
where I sought
truth,
goodness,
beauty,
and found the opposite
of those things—
in that
dorm in the city
where I could not
walk
without fear
of meeting the one
who defrauded my heart—
in that city
I had entertainment,
and amenities,
space,
all the makings
of a good home,
but in that city
I never had peace.

I hate this house,
which exposes

so many
bleeding,
aching
parts of me
that I don't
want to see.

But after living here,
discovering
beautiful things
amongst the ashes
of my anger and hatred,
I have come to
appreciate this house
which I could once
only see
as my adversary.

Here in this house,
full of flaws,
failed dreams,
disappointments,
unbearable realities,
I found myself
able to walk outside
freely,
without fear

of him reaching me here.
Able to confront
the wounds
carved deep inside
of me
in a place
both heartbreaking
and beautiful.

Here in this broken down,
cast-off house
I discovered that
joy can be found
in the unlikeliest
of places.

Here in this discarded,
overlooked house
I unearthed that
when something beautiful
comes from something ugly,
it is like the popping of a corn kernel.
It unfolds from the inside out
so that what is beautiful is apparent and enjoyed
while the kernel of ugliness remains, now hidden but present,
not wasted, not forgotten, not invalidated.

But instead,
swallowed with the beauty.

Sitting with these
traumatized memories
and tattered dreams,
I have learned to
love this house
and learned to
love you,
my own self,
whom I once blamed
for my tragedy.

## Washed Away

Sky was dark,
and sea even darker.
Rain torrented from the heavens,
the sun sealed up and locked away
behind the clouds.

On the shore
were two—
a woman weeping,
a man pleading.
She stepped ever further away
while he tried to reach closer.
Her words raged at him like thunder;
his wicked off her like the rain.

"I can't do this anymore."
Every time she set free
the pain in her heart,
the tide inched further up the shore.

"Please, don't do this."
He tried to move her
out of the path of the surging tide,

but she was so far from him
that her lifelong friend had become
a passing stranger.

She wanted nothing more
than to fully unleash her grief.
He clawed and clutched
at the ache in his heart,
knowing that one so dear suffered
and she would not suffer him
to console her.

She stared emptily
out at the swelling sea.
"Life has broken my heart," she rasped.
"Trampled on it,
torn it to pieces,
and you stand there,
trying to cheer me up,
as if it were truly that simple.
I don't want anything more
to do with you."

She started to walk
toward the sea.

"Don't go,"
he began.

But she wouldn't
even let him finish.

"I don't want to hear
about how my present pain
will all have been worth it
when I see how happy I am
in the future."

She walked along the shore,
her dress, blue as her tears,
billowing in the gale
as she stooped down.
She began to weep anew
when she couldn't see
her own reflection in the choppy waters.
All that she was
had been utterly lost,
drowned in sorrow.

"You say things will get better soon,
but I can't even imagine
what better looks like,
or see it on the horizon.
It's as far removed from my reality
as Atlantis.
Thinking of a vague promise
that life will be better in the future

doesn't give me any hope.
So I'll say again,
don't tell me
that the pain I feel now,
which is so present to me,
is nothing compared to
the happiness I may feel in the future.
That doesn't comfort me.

"And don't tell me
that my pain is
making me a better person,
giving me a new perspective, or
helping me to heal others
who will suffer the same things I am.
I don't care about wisdom
or empathy
or personal growth.
I just want
my pain to end.

"Don't tell me
that after death
I will never cry again
and my every tear
will be wiped away.
What about my tears now?

Why can't someone wipe those away?
Why can't I be happy now?"

She looked at him
with anger and hurt
dug into her face.
He stayed utterly
still and silent,
so she turned back
to the water.

Where she could see nothing before,
now she saw a face.
A smiling, laughing face.
Her uncle.
She thought about him after his surgery
for his cancer.
Laughing and joking with his family.
Surgery, cancer,
laughter, smiles.
These were words
she could not reconcile.

"What am I missing?"
she said,
staring at those faces
in the water.

"We are all in pain
 but I am weeping,
 and they are smiling.
 What is the difference
 between them
 and me?"

"You asked what you were missing.
 Gratitude.
 That is the difference
 between them
 and you."

Her eyes widened
and she started to shake,
so he moved closer to her,
but she moved away.

"How am I supposed to
 be grateful for suffering?"
 she shouted,
 her voice as raw
 as the peals of thunder
 all around them.

"No, not that.
 Gratitude for what is good."

She looked away from him
and out
toward the endlessly raging sea.
"It feels like there is no longer
anything good."

He gently put his hand
on her shoulder
and moved her attention
back to him.
"Don't look your sorrow
in the eye.
It will knock you off your feet
and sweep you into
a universe of tears.

"If you didn't know
anything about the tide,
you would see it reaching further
and further
up the shore,
and you would think that soon it would swallow
the whole world,
that there would never again be
even a patch
of dry land.

"But don't look
at the tide.
Don't look at the land
that's being washed away.
Climb uphill to higher ground
and look at the land
that yet remains.
See the trees and the flowers
that still exist
up above the beach.
If the things that once brought you joy
have been washed away with the tide,
don't waste your time
trying to chase the water away
and reverse the tide
with your little bucket.
Walk further inland.
Find new, beautiful land
that brings you new joy.

"If you can't yet figure out how
to be grateful for the past joys
that the rising tide has washed away,
don't despair.
Turn your eyes away from the tide
and find yourself a new patch of land

to be grateful for
and rejoice over.

"Focus your gaze on whatever is good,
whatever is lovely,
whatever is joyful,
whatever is noble,
whatever is beautiful.
Much of the world is indeed
covered in water,
but there will always be land.
Even Noah's dove
was able to find an olive branch
after the whole world was flooded.

"And I know you are hurting too much
to believe me now,
but one day,
the tide will recede.
And all the land
that you thought
was washed away
forever
you will reclaim,
and untold treasure
will be found

where once there was only
the watery deep."

He held out his hand
to embrace her in a hug.

"In this moment," she whispered,
her thundering anger
giving way to words
light and gentle as the rain,
"I am grateful
to have such a dear friend
who did not give up on me
when I had already
given up
on both myself and him."

She looked up at him,
then closed her eyes,
leaning into him,
as he held her
between his arms.
He smiled
as she smiled
and her fountain of tears
finally,
finally,
began to dry.

"Look," he said.
She turned
in his arms,
and saw
that the rain had stopped,
and the sun was free
to shine
with radiant glory.

Looking down
at their feet
and the water
that swirled between their toes
and lapped at their ankles,
she shifted in his arms
to lean back against him
and let his weight
support her.

With a serene smile
on her face
that he could not see,
she murmured,
"I think I have found
my patch of dry land."

## Life, drowning candle

wick submerged neck deep
in its own sweat, keeps burning.

## Ashes, Ashes

Ashes, ashes,
we all fall
down.

So why
get back
up?

You are dust and to dust
you shall
return.

If then I am dust
sooner let me
go.

Cinderella, why go to the ball at all
if you knew your life would fall back to
rags?

All else seems dull and blunt
compared with the sharp blade of
death.

And why should I bother trying

to climb from this pit when in the end I'll only
fail?

Ashes, ashes,
we all fall down—cease your vain hope of
rising.

Ashes, ashes,
you are bound
by your nothingness,
but I am not.

It is truly a law of nature
that what goes up
must come
down,
yet it is no less true
that what dies
must rise again.

Does not the sun
fall down every day
and get back up again
no worse for wear?

And the seasons—
nature loses her royal robe
in winter,

yet finds it again
good as new
in spring.

Look at the seeds
which fall from the tree
to be buried in the dark earth,
yet given time
they sprout up
and grow toward the heavens.

And the waves,
do they not dash themselves
to destruction
upon the rocks?
Yet scarce before
you can even mourn them,
they return,
playfully rushing again to their doom.
You see,
death does not disturb the waves,
for they know
death is but a revolving door
that leads again to more life.

Ashes, ashes
do indeed fall down.

Dust to dust
does indeed return.

All that lives and loves
does indeed die.

Lives are upended,
hearts are broken,

But death is a part of life,
not life merely a part of death.

The ash is a part of the fire,
not the fire part of ash.

And dust a part of man,
not man a part of dust.

Ashes, ashes,
do not fear falling down
for in the falling
is half the getting up.

# The Butterfly House

*A story about how to move forward for those who feel left behind.*

I watch a butterfly land on a pond in the front yard, creating ripples on the water. Once, I would have called it a beautiful sight, but now, it just leads my thoughts in a direction that they have been traveling in all too often already.

Have you ever noticed how even the slightest movement can upset our peace? A delicate breeze stirring can startle off the butterfly on our nose, or a spark can burn down a whole forest. I know people who have trouble finding meaning in life, but as for me, I've discovered that even our littlest actions matter entirely too much. Even the lightest gesture can become unbearably heavy.

The honk of the horn from my parents' car stops my train of thought before it can steamroll me like a helpless victim tied to railroad tracks in old western movies. I wave goodbye to my parents from the front porch of my aunt and uncle's house.

"We'll see you in two weeks, Mateo," my mom lowers the window to call out as the car begins to roll out of the gravel driveway. Will I really see them again, though? Such simple words of farewell, which I would have once thought nothing of, now fall like a stone to the pit of my stomach.

"Take good care of yourself, and don't give your aunt and uncle a hard time." My dad waves goodbye out of the driver-side window, and then they are gone, leaving me with the dreadful weight upon my shoulders that this may be the last time I ever see or speak to them again. It wouldn't be the first time this would happen without me knowing.

I tell my aunt and uncle that I'll be inside soon. I walk around the back of the house, the overgrown grass and weeds scratching my bare legs below the knee where my shorts end. Off to one corner of the yard, a butterfly house stands above all the wild foliage, perched atop a wooden pole driven sturdily into the ground. The wood on both the stake and the house has begun to rot and collapse in some places. Paint chips have flaked off all over the butterfly house, and the color that does remain is desaturated from age, no longer attracting the attention of butterflies with the vibrant hues that I remember.

Things are no longer how I thought they would be. When you're happy, you never stop to think that there will come a time when you will feel sad. Yet once the sadness comes, you can hardly imagine ever feeling happy again.

When I built this butterfly house, I wasn't thinking about how it would one day fall apart and all my hard work would go to ruin, as if it had never been at all. On that bright summer day, all I felt was pride at how beautiful a job my cousin and I had done. Excitement at the thought of wild butterflies living in something I had made.

Now, it is a broken and dead thing, and I don't see how it could hold life ever again. It can't. That is what dead means, after all.

Unable to look at the remains of such a happy time any longer, I head inside the house.

Uncle Charles and Aunt Edna are already sitting down at the eat-in table in the kitchen for dinner. They haven't touched their food yet, and there is a third plate laid out for me.

"Mateo, we never did get to sing you happy birth—"

"That's okay, Aunt Edna," I say.

My uncle tells me that they've had my present here waiting for me, that they didn't think it was appropriate to give it to me after they saw me at the funeral and they didn't want to mail it in case it got lost. So they kept it these past six months, waiting for me to come.

When I open the box, there's a carving knife inside, with my name engraved on the grip.

"Just like Parker," I whisper.

I always wanted to be as good at woodworking as my older cousin, but this isn't how it was supposed to go—me with a beautiful knife and fresh wood and no one here to teach me. Me here and him there and the butterfly house we made together rotting outside.

I thank them for the gift and for dinner, which we eat mostly in silence. It's not the same as the dinners we used to have here when I visited for the summers, with me and Parker laughing loudly and the adults shaking their heads fondly at us. I push most of the food around my plate to make it look like my mind is at least a little bit present, and after a sufficient length of time for a meal has passed, I tell them that I'm tired from the drive and I'm going to bed early tonight. It's apparent from their body language that they're worried about me, but they just don't know what to say or do. I've seen that expression too many times these past six months. I do my best to ignore it.

The room that I always stay in when I come to visit, right across the hall from Parker's, looks exactly the way I left it the last time I stayed here. As I change into my pajamas and climb into the bed, I cannot help but think that even though it looks the same, it could not feel more different. I'm afraid to close my eyes, to end up back in that place that keeps making me an unwilling guest every night for the past six months. But I do drift off to sleep, and then I find myself in my pajamas chasing after a car as it pulls out of a driveway, with headlights down the road in the distance.

"No, you can't!" I wave my arms back and forth wildly to try to catch the driver's attention. "You can't come here!

"You can't come see me," I plead, jumping away from the road before the car runs over me. But I know from other dreams I've had, ones where I don't jump out of the way, that it will just drive straight through me. "If you come visit me here, you'll die," I say softly, sitting hopelessly on the edge of the sidewalk, watching as the car drives headlong into its doom.

When the inevitable happens, I bolt upright in bed, sweat soaking my arms and my face. At some point, I must have kicked out of my quilt, because it's strewn halfway off the edge of the bed and halfway on the floor, and my sheets are crumpled.

My parents thought that if they sent me away, the nightmares wouldn't find me, that out in the country with dirt paths, I wouldn't be plagued by dreams of car crashes on city roads. Or maybe they just couldn't bear to mourn one child and watch helplessly as the other one is terrorized by bad dreams every night.

I wish I could go back to that day. Nothing has been right since then, and I can't keep myself from thinking, *if I could just change one thing...*

I know I won't be able to sleep anymore tonight, so I put on a light jacket and go to sit in the backyard and stare at the butterfly house as the sun rises.

*And then there's you, Parker. Maybe if we hadn't played so many shooting games you wouldn't have decided to grow up and join the army. Maybe you would still be here with aunt and uncle, and the butterfly house wouldn't look like this. You'd have been here to take care of it. We'd have been here to fix it, together.*

Now, all that's left of my cousin is this falling-apart house, and of my sister, nightmares. It's just me, alone on my own. As I so often find myself doing lately, I turn to my memories—the only place I can still see either of them.

I didn't think that something so simple as waking up to find a butterfly in the house could make me that happy. I ran through the garden and the flowers, laughing and sticking my nose in the air, hoping that my new friend would land on it. I remember it was so hard to hold still. I was petrified—worried even my breathing would scare it away. I remember Parker laughing at my silliness so hard that he had to clutch his stomach, and I fussed at him for being so loud that he might startle the butterfly and cause it to fly off.

Wondering how long it has been since this decrepit thing has attracted any visitors since that day, I pick up the butterfly house. The only place this thing belongs now is in the trash. Nothing as beautiful as a butterfly would want to live in such an ugly, worn-down place. As I'm peering into the hole, trying to make sure there's no life inside before I throw the house away, an orange and red butterfly flies out at me like sparks popping from a fire, and I stumble backwards in surprise.

"Two-eyes! What do you think you're doing?"

The flame-colored butterfly hovers at my eye level, scowling at me with a gaze far more intimidating than I ever would have expected from a butterfly.

"I'm very sorry," I mumble. "I didn't know anyone lived here."

My apology only seems to anger her further. "This is my home! I have lived here my whole life cycle. My mother, father, broth—" she stops mid-sentence and scoffs, folding her arms across her chest. "Who are you, two-eyes, and why are you here? No one has come out this far into the garden in generations."

"My name is Mateo. With my cousin I built this house, many years ago." I try to smile at her, but I fear it is more of a grimace when I meet her harsh eyes. "And what is your name, compound-eyes?"

I sit down cross-legged in the weeds and the grass, and the red-orange butterfly unfolds the breadth of her wings in the palm of my hands, hovering just above them.

"Mother and father called me Hesper, because I reminded them of the evening sun. From my great ancestor Hestia all the way down to my brother Heph and I, fire has always burned brightly in our line. But the flames have all gone out, and now it is only me."

For the briefest moment, when she told me her name, her eyes softened into wistfulness, losing something of their ferocity and wrath. But when she asked me what I was doing with her house, that fierce, intimidating gaze returned.

"I was going to take it and throw it away," I admitted. "It is awful and sad, and I can't stand seeing it every time I look out my bedroom window. Every time my eyes fall on it, all I can think is how everything has gone and changed and left me behind, and all I can do is cry and wish for life to go back to how it was. When I was happy."

To my surprise, she agreed. "It is an awful and sad little house."

"Then if you don't like it, why do you stay? You are a lovely butterfly who feeds on beautiful flowers. You, at least, can fly away from such ugly things."

She shakes her head. "Even a life of drinking nectar is not always so sweet. I will never leave this garden. This house is where my brother lived his whole life, and I with him, and these fields, now overgrown, are where he died. This is all I have left of him. Please, you cannot dare throw it away!"

I promised Hesper that I would not touch her family's house. Even living in such a state of poverty and disrepair, creatures cling to life there in the dying wood of that old house. While I know my sister is gone and never coming home, seeing a flicker of warmth and vibrancy, no matter how faint, gives me hope that my cousin is okay. That one day he will walk through the front gate and come teach me the secrets of woodworking, and things might almost feel normal again.

My aunt sees me sitting outside in the soft early morning light, and she steps outside through the patio door, inviting me to come inside for a mug of steaming hot chocolate and then to help her cook for today. As she hands me the warm mug, I look at the kitchen counter already filled with ingredients—alfredo sauce, boxes of pasta noodles, shakers full of seasonings and spices, a head of broccoli, a bag of shrimp on the top shelf of the fridge.

The thought of being in the kitchen makes me a little sick to my stomach. I haven't had much of an appetite since Wittiveen died, but, not wanting to be rude, I silently nod in agreement.

"Teo, listen," she says after we were both quiet for a while. "I know that after you lose someone you love, it can feel like you're in a dream where even lifting one foot to take a step feels as slow and heavy as molasses."

I sigh. That is exactly how I feel. Stuck. Trapped. Frozen. Setting the dish rag I used to wash my empty mug aside on the counter, I turn around to look at her. "How can you move forward when you feel like that? When you can't stop thinking about it?"

She is cutting the shells off the tops of the shrimps, so she does not turn to look at me. "For me, it helped to do what I like to call 'little human things.'" I can hear the smile in her voice. "You know, those chores we drag our feet and groan about doing when everything is all right and we have so many things we would like better to do. Folding laundry, dusting cabinets, shining old shoes, washing dishes, making beds, buying groceries. I believe these awfully boring little human things are a gift for those of us who don't quite know how to move forward. We do them all our lives, from the time we are children, so they feel easy and familiar and safe, even when nothing else in our life does. When we do these little boring human things that we know we need to, it saves us from having to think too far into the future and finding ourselves paralyzed by worrying about what we should do or how we can move forward. We are so used to doing these little human things, repeating them day in and day out of our lives, that our bodies know what to do without being told by our brain, without having to push through the molasses in our heads. And by the time we set out to do them, we find the chores are already done, and in our own way, we have moved forward."

I hold the strainer over the sink as Aunt pours in the boiled noodles from the pot.

"Mateo, my dear, until such time as the molasses and inertia melts away from all your thoughts and actions, until such time as you find you can hope and dream without fear of the future again, you can stay here and just boil noodles with me."

For perhaps the first time since she died, I find myself smiling. I thought that it would be hard to do, that it would hurt, that perhaps I would have forgotten how. I thought that smiling in a world where she no longer existed would feel different somehow. I thought that maybe I would feel guilty. But it feels as natural and good to me as making my favorite food, shrimp alfredo.

I spend the rest of the day helping Aunt and Uncle around the house with chores, and by the time the end of the day comes, for the first time in the months since my sister died, I am able to sleep peacefully.

When I wake up in the morning and see torrential sheets of rain pouring from the sky outside, I slip on my shoes and run out to the butterfly house, grabbing an umbrella on the way.

"Hesper?" I whisper, opening up the umbrella over both me and the house.

Moments later, a little fire flutters out of one of the slits. "Are all humans this nosy, or is it just you, two-eyes?"

I chuckle into the back of my hand. While I initially found her prickliness off-putting, it is starting to grow on me, like the twang of a kiwi that is somehow still sweet.

"I never thought about it until now, but with all the holes in the wood, you must get soaked and freezing cold every time it rains. I..." Could I really do this again, after all these years? Could I do it without him?

"Let me build you a new butterfly house," I say.

"No," Hesper says.

"But why? You're sure to catch a cold from all these summer storms."

She turns her back to me. "It would be entirely fitting of what I deserve."

"Hesper, I don't understand."

"My momma always said the same thing to me when I was little. 'Don't play outside in the rain, Hesper! You'll catch your death out there!' But it wasn't mine I caught. It was my brother's. I ignored her and played in the rain anyway one day. I got sick, and my brother caught my cold from me, and he never got better."

"Hesper—"

She flips around to glare at me with startling grace and speed. "It is *my* fault Heph died! Just go away—you can't understand!"

A birthday party, with balloons and presents on the table and cake, flashes painfully in my memories.

"Actually," I murmur, staring down at my shoes, "I can."

"I am not in the mood for riddles, two-eyes," she barks.

"My sister's name was Wittiveen, and it's my fault she died. On my birthday."

All the anger and the fire drain out of her face, as though they have been washed down by the falling rain. "Oh, Mateo, I did not know. I am so sorry."

"I turned 14 this winter, and she drove all the way home from her college to be with me on my birthday. The party had just started when I realized we forgot to pick up some of my favorite strawberry lemonade while we were at the store yesterday, so I asked Wittiveen if she could run out to the shop down the street and get some.

"When half an hour passed and she didn't come home, we started calling her, but she didn't answer. My dad and I took his car and went to look for her, and we found her little red car t-boned by a green one not far from our house. The firefighters and paramedics were cutting her out of the car. We followed them to the hospital, but she died there later that night."

I continue to hold the umbrella over us, staring down at my shoes. Hesper comes to perch on my shoulder.

"I wish I had not gone and played in the rain," Hesper says quietly.

"I wish I hadn't asked for strawberry lemonade," I reply, in just as quiet a voice.

"I want to show you something," Hesper says, and disappears into the butterfly house before returning a moment later and dropping something in my hand. It looks like a salmon-colored scale, shimmering like lake water in the sunlight.

"It's quite beautiful. What is it?"

She smiles and there is a soft warmth that lights her face, like the calming glow of a candle. "When we were kids, I always complained that Heph had prettier wings than me, so one day he gave me a scale from one of his." She laughs, shaking her head fondly.

"I see why it's so precious to you. My sister got me a fresh piece of cedar wood for my birthday, but in the time since then, I never knew what I could carve that would be worthy of the last gift she ever gave me."

Hesper's eyes widen. "Mateo, I have an idea!"

She looks almost shy to tell me her idea at first, but with enough coaxing and reassurance from me, she finally does. She tells me she wants the garden to be beautiful again, like it once was, as a tribute to her brother. And she wants me to carve a new butterfly house, with a special place to display Heph's scale inside.

"It is time this place lived again," she says.

"And you too?" I ask.

"And *us* too."

Since our conversation, I have been thinking that I want to use Wittiveen's cedar to carve the butterfly house. To carve something beautiful with the knife Parker and Aunt and Uncle got me, and for life to go on living inside the wood Witteveen had given me—I think it would be a fitting tribute to both of them.

But there is still one thing holding me back.

It takes me a few more days, but I finally work up the courage to start a conversation that I was never able to since the day she died. I lie out in the grass in the garden with my cell phone sitting on my chest, and Hesper hovering nearby me.

"Hi, mom, it's me."

"Teo, honey, it's good to hear from you. How has your time with Edna and Charles been going?"

"Really good." I smile. "Hey mom, can I ask you a question?"

Hesper flies near my ear, her wings tickling me, and asks, "Are you sure I should be listening to this?"

"Absolutely," I whisper back.

"Are you mad at me… about Wittiveen?"

There's a sigh on the other end of the line, a sad one. "Oh, my dear son. Is that what you have believed all this time?"

"But it *is* my fault! If I hadn't asked for the strawberry lemonade, she wouldn't have been on the road at all then! How could you not be angry?"

"Trust me, Mateo. I am not angry with you at all, nor do I blame you," she says gently. "I am sorrowful that my daughter and your sister is gone. Sometimes I even feel angry that she died. But I never, ever feel angry at you, and I know that could she tell you so, Wittiveen would say the same."

I glance over at Hesper to make sure she is still listening.

"My beloved son, this is a lesson I did not expect you to have to learn so soon, but you must know this. When people die of accidents, of illnesses, of circumstances, we must not blame ourselves. We must not think that we have been unfairly robbed of much more time with them than we could have had. For the truth is, though that time is not known to us beforehand, everyone has their time to die. As humans, we are blessed with the knowledge and capability to extend and even save lives. Insomuch as we are able to preserve life, we should, but to hold on to life and time indefinitely is not within our power. For no matter how much we know, or how perfectly we may strive to live, we are mortal. When a person dies, that too is a part of living life on this earth—something that in the end, no matter what you do or did, you cannot prevent. To think on what could be is the joy of the dreamer, but to think of what could have been is an exercise in unreality and futility.

"Mateo, dearest son, I would much rather you spend your shooting stars and your eyelashes and your dreams wishing for things that can still be changed."

I felt warm tears stream down my face, tears of relief as much as of grief.

I am amazed by how serene and clear-headed my mom is about all this. Meanwhile I have been worrying myself into knots, and I imagine Hesper feels much the same, her anger at herself plain to see. Plain to me, because I recognize it as the same guilt-laden frustration I have been feeling within myself. That's why I wanted her to listen to my phone call. I thought that if whatever my mom had to say could help me, it could help her, too.

"I think I'm ready to create something new and beautiful out of everything Parker and Wittiveen left behind," I say, as I set to work with Parker's knife and Wittiveen's block of wood.

"I think it will turn out wonderfully," Hesper comments. She has been smiling so much more these days, and I suppose I have been as well.

"I hope so. I'm not very good at carving. Parker could have done it better."

"That may be so, but he could not have done it like you. To him, it would just be a butterfly house. To you, to us, it's so much more."

It takes me a couple of days to build the house and paint it, and Hesper remains by my side the entire time.

"It's finished," I say.

There Hesper and I stand, looking at the work we made together. The home fashioned of wood, scales, the memories of loved ones left behind, and our hopes of moving forward while still looking back.

"I tried to recreate the original house, but I know it's not the same," I sigh.

"I think it's even more beautiful than the old one," Hesper says.

I've always thought since the day my sister died that our little choices matter too much. That I shouldn't be burdened with the responsibility of knowing that I live in such a world where my desire for a glass of lemonade could kill someone.

"Thank you, Mateo. Your sister and cousin would be proud of you if they could see this, and I know my brother would be, too."

But now I see that our little choices matter just enough, and I find it amazing that a little house made for a little butterfly in a little piece of countryside could mean so much.

## Did flowers grow in Carthage

over the salted earth?

Because I saw them growing
in the scorched earth
of my heart.

## I DISCOVERED

in the valley
that life down here
is still livable.

I discovered that
having my plans wrecked
and ruined
is awful,
but not as awful
as I had imagined.

It is deep down here
but not as deep as I thought
it would be
from the place
up there at the top of the mountain.

I found
down here
the immensely relieving
truth
that it is perfectly okay
to be weak.

That
imperfection
is just
the underside
of the tapestry
of perfection,

That imperfection
is the stitches
that hold together
the lovely beauty
we find in perfection.

I discovered
down here
that life still looks quite beautiful
from last place.

I didn't expect
to find
happiness here.

I didn't plan
on fireflies
flittering
gently
through the darkness
of the valley.

## I WANT TO BE

the flower bearer
for you

Except instead of
strewing petals
at your feet
as you walk down the aisle

I want to
cast little reminders
of all the beauty
that exists within this world
as you walk through life

Making each of your steps
through the somber darkness
even the smallest bit
brighter

## Way Lights

Darkness lives all around.
Sight skips like stones
on water,
guiding me one step
but then, no further.

I live my life
clinging to the light.
In the black water
all around, who knows
what lurks down there?

How far this path
will go, I'll know
only at its end.
Another route out there,
not worth the daring
to wander the dark.

Don't travel by yourself
or surely you'll find
The Bogeyman. He's out there
with the demons, but
I'm my own Devil.

Jay W. Song

*Keep to the light*
is easier said than done
when darkness hides
inside you.

I didn't expect that
the way lights would find
me.
They came to me
in the drowning dark.

One light before me
became two,
two became three
until a web of way lights
spread out before me,
leading me out of myself,
guiding me one step
at a time
into a bigger, brighter world.

Like a horse led to water,
they showed me I could drink.
The way lights showed me an oasis
where I had seen the barren desert
of my own loneliness.

The way lights held my hand

and taught me
we are all devils unto ourselves
but angels unto others.

I am darkness to myself
but a way light to others.

You do not have to wander in the dark.
Look down the hill
into the glittering valley
and let the way lights
of kindred souls
guide you home.

## To the man who

offered me the last
shopping cart at Costco
when you could have
easily taken it for yourself
and thought nothing of me:
thank you
for quietly restoring
a little bit of my faith
in humanity.

To the woman
at the antique store
who decided to give me a discount
for no reason
other than to simply be kind:
thank you
for reminding me
that no action,
no matter how small,
is without value.

## When I was a child

my dad always told me,
"Never say you can't do something."

I never understood
why that mattered
until I stopped
saying it
and instead saw all that I accomplished.

# I Am Dream

Starting out as a little thought
no bigger than a crumb forgotten in your mind,
but you cannot forget me.
Growing now to the size of a bean—
I am a seed that will grow without nourishment.
I will grow in the dark.
I will grow in the pain.
I will grow in the sunshine.
I will grow in the rain.
I am a seed that will grow, but into what, you do not know.
Stomp on me,
tear off my leaves,
burn me,
pull me from the ground,
but I will still grow.
Because I am a dream.

## Well

See me.
I am a well,
but no matter how deeply
I reach down into myself,
I can find no water.

See me.
My stones are fractured.
Moss grows on me, and choking vines.
My rope is frayed to a strand
and my crank—rusted into place.
Even if there was water in me,
you could not draw it.

See me.
I am unwell.
For I am purposeless
if I cannot do that for which I was made.

See me.
My bottomless depths curse the rain
for even a flood shows me
how empty I am.
The cracks in my stones run so wide

that any water you fill me with
pours back out.
There is nothing that can fill me.
My existence is insatiable
and futile.

See me, the empty well.
See me, the grieved unwell.
See me, my own end I clearly spell.
It is not well with me.

Having no use,
I should be unmade.
I should be undone.

Mourning my emptiness,
meaninglessness,
purposelessness,
reliving the days when I had fullness,
and life,
and use—

Clink.
A sound disturbs my reverie.
I see a child peering down into me,
their hand full of coins brown and silver.

Clink.
"I wish that I could be an astronaut when I grow up."

The coin settles
at the bottom of my sightless depths.
It is the first thing
that does not leak back out of me.

The wish settles
somewhere even deeper within me.
It is the first thing
that makes me feel full again.

I see
the nascent glimpse
of new life,
glimmering like stars
that reveal their hidden presence
upon descent of night.

I hold my breath,
shimmering with excitement
as more people appear,
filling me with their coins and wishes.

Jay W. Song

Clink.
"I wish my mom would get better soon."
Clink.
"I wish to get the job, so I can move closer to my family."
Clink.
"I wish to find the love of my life."

As the dry depths within me
fill with the tangible embodiment
of so many hopes and dreams,
for the first time in my existence
I find myself not leaking,
but overflowing.

My mossy stone heart—
so firm, now gentle.
So scarred, now beautiful.

My ravenous well
now rich and abundant.
These bottomless depths
overflowing as though they were the most
shallow of pools.

Wishes and dreams
have given me, the unwell, purpose.

## Becoming the Dawn

Having found
a new way of my existence,
I have been remade.
I have been redone.

See me.
I am a wishing well.
Reach down into me,
and find your dreams.

## My Name is Creativity

Hop aboard my train
I'll take you where you want to go
Mountains high or valleys low
My name is Creativity.

Jump into my house
I'll be a roof above your head
And give you dreams as you lie in bed
My name is Creativity.

Raise me to the skies
I'll shield you from the rains
Drown away your earthly pains
My name is Creativity.

Put your hand through mine
I'll make sure you don't fall
And walk with you through it all
My name is Creativity.

Follow behind me in the night
I will lead you to the light
Hold me close, hold me tight
My name is Creativity.

Draw upon me in your time of need
I will be your source of power
And help you through your darkest hour
My name is Creativity.

Bottle me up into a pen
And I will flow back out again
I am what makes you human
My name is Creativity.

Strike me down upon paper
I will serve as a window into your soul
Expressing yourself helps make you whole
My name is Creativity.

Take me with you when you die
I will be there as you heave your last sigh
And fly with you to the gates in the sky
My name is Creativity.

# Art

Wet paint stains
coat your hands
like a second skin,
the colors as diverse as your heart.

You raise your hand to cover your mouth
as you laugh,
and the color wheel smears across your lips.
Somehow, it suits you.

You taught me how
to see again.
I saw once, as a child,
but I had gone blind.

Beauty lives in a drop of rain
or a million,
in a single flower
or a garden.

Meaning abounds in both a splatter of paint
and a full canvas.
One is random, the other orderly.
Both are human.

Black ink tattoos
etch the language
of heavenly gods
into your skin.

You are the scribe of the universe,
recording her story wherever it will fit.
When you run out of paper, you use your body,
a finite book for an infinite story.

You reminded me
how to feel.
I did feel once, as a child,
but I had fallen out of practice.

The gems of emotions
glitter brightly
within the dark cave
of imperfection.

Eternal things hide within
the bodies of mayflies,
and everything that appears constant
is always changing.

Silence rests
atop your skin,

but beneath it
sings the universe.

You are the voice of the mute gods,
carrying their essence within
and slowly dispersing it
back into a deaf world.

You returned to me
life's sound.
I heard it once, as a child,
but I had lost its melody.

The ashes of the universe
slumber deep within us,
awaiting earth's song
to rekindle themselves.

The world is not as silent as it seems.
We cannot hear it,
for the tune it sings
matches the music within us.

Wrinkles and age
mar my skin
and wear it down
to buried bones.

## Becoming the Dawn

Life and time
steal my sight,
dull my heart,
and blanket my ears in silence.

While you reside within me,
you restore me.
I was a child once,
and a child again you make me.

I considered myself wise once,
but you have taught and teach aplenty.
If it is knowledge about ourselves we seek,
then look not in the numbers or in the stars,

but in ourselves and in our art.

## Forsaking fair stages

of theatres and opera houses,
I dance beauty in the mud.
The good earth humbles me,
freeing me
from the snare of perfection.

## Your feet have walked the soft grass

and the hard paths.
Even the seas
saw you pass.

Your feet have climbed hills
and rested by pools of water
within the desert as life stills
in the evening silence.

Your feet have trudged mountains
rugged and cruel,
sacred and glorious,
bathed in blood or light.

If you look back
at all the places
you have walked,
climbed,
and trudged
through,

you will see
that you
are a warrior.

## A Bluebird's Song

Oh,
how can I sing
when it is so dark?

It is like
I am trapped,
and they have thrown
a black sheet over my cage.

I am
the only bird
who has never seen the sun.
No one knows my pain
because I am hidden in the dark.
No one understands.

Oh,
how can I sing
when I have nothing to sing about,
and no one to sing for?

Everyone tells me
bluebirds have the loveliest songs,
and therefore I,

being silent,
am all the more a tragedy.

After all,
what is the point
of a bluebird
that cannot sing?

A bluebird with a sheet over its cage, a young girl under a sheet on her bed—to her the two images were perfectly analogous. The bird would never be able to leave its cage, and she would never be able to leave her bed.

When she rolled onto her side, her gaze fell in view of the baby monitor sitting on the nightstand beside her bed, a humiliating reminder of her imprisonment. As she coughed, she reached for the glass of water on the stand, but it was empty. The clock on the wall read 2:39 AM—she could not bear to wake either of her parents just for a glass of water. Surely she could at least do that much, such a simple little thing as walking down the hall to the kitchen, by herself. Flinging the sheets back, she gingerly moved her legs to the side of the bed, her feet resting a little above the floor. It wasn't that her legs were paralyzed, after all, so walking was still a possibility. At least, that was what she told herself. Last month she had so much pain in her legs that they nearly gave out, and the second time the pain had come back, they did. She had been bedridden since then, but maybe with all the rest of the past few weeks, her legs would be able to support her again.

Delicately, like a feather falling to the grass, she put her toes to the ground, and then the sole of her foot, and then the heel. So far so good. Her palms began to sweat as she pushed up off the bed and started to put weight on her legs. She did not even manage to stand fully upright on her own before she collapsed and fell, bumping the nightstand and sending the empty glass shattering onto the floor.

She did not make a sound. She just smiled in self-pity and sobbed silently as she heard her mother call her name and come running.

Her mother cried out as she saw her on the floor. Kneeling beside her, she helped her raise herself into an upright position.

"What happened? Are you hurt?"

"No, Mama, I'm okay."

Her mother looked at her the way only someone who has raised a child all their life can, with eyes that gently, but stubbornly said, *I know you.*

The young girl let her mother help lift her back up into the bed, and when she was settled under the sheets again, she slid over to make room for Mama to sit.

"I tried to get up and walk," she mumbled.

Her mother's eyes were empty of judgment, and full of love. Her voice overflowed with compassion and concern as she simply asked, "Why?"

The young girl stayed silent for a long time, staring at her legs stretched out under the pastel pink sheets. Tears began to pour out of her eyes like water from a dark grey cloud that had long held off releasing its rain but could no longer keep back the burden.

The rain that fell was heavy but quiet, unaccompanied by dramatic peals of thunder or forceful strikes of lightning. "I'm just so tired.

"I can't walk anymore. I can't even go get a glass of water on my own. I'm trapped in this bed, staring out the window at a world I should be a part of.

"Sometimes I feel perfectly normal, and sometimes I feel like I'm eighty years old. I never know when the pain will come next. It steals over me as silently and mercilessly as a wolf and drags me away by the throat.

"My hair—" for this long she had maintained the quiet composure of the rain, but now her voice began to crescendo in frustration and panic like rumblings of distant thunder crawling nearer. "My hair is coming out! It's all over my pillow and my clothes. It comes out when I run my hands through it. Tufts of it come through when I try to comb it."

She turned away from Mama, pulling her knees to her chest and wrapping her arms around them. She was quiet for a long time, as though she wanted to say more but couldn't find the words. Like a bone in the back of her throat, she couldn't get all her suffering out, and she struggled to breathe.

She sighed. "Don't worry, Ma, I'll be fine. I'm just tired. I'm sorry I worried you. Go back to sleep."

Her mother looked at her with pained eyes. She knew Mama suffered, in her own way, just as much as she did from her mysterious illness.

"I can stay with you until morning," Mama offered.

The young girl held up a very old stuffed bunny with patches and button eyes that had been re-sewn many times. "I've got Quincy to keep watch," she smiled.

Mama tried again. "Tell you a bedtime story?"

The young girl, really too old for bedtime stories and stuffed animals, looked at Mama long and hard for a moment, and then burst into laughter as she said, "Of course."

Mama couldn't heal all the pain she felt inside and out, but she could make her smile. And as she always told her when she was a child, "Smiles are the best medicine."

Yet what her mother did not teach her, what she learned as an adult, was that smiles are also the best disguise.

There are birds
who can mimic
the songs of
other creatures.

Lovely as
they may be,
those songs
aren't written
for bluebirds.

If all
a bluebird does
is sing the song
of a lark
then of what good
is a bluebird?

How does the bluebird
learn to sing?
Does its mother teach it?
Do all bluebirds
sing the same song?

Or is a song
something special,
something unique
that develops deep within
the heart?

When a bluebird sings
from whence comes her song?
When she sings
does she serenade the sky
with an untaught tune?

A silent bluebird—
perhaps she is just waiting
to discover her song.

Morning came soon—the rambunctious April sun playfully jumping through the window— and it pained her that she could not go out and play with those lovely sunbeams. There was not only no possibility, but no reason, to get out of bed. She had been sick for a long time, a year, and it only kept getting worse. Doctors were not sure if or when she would improve, and so she had to withdraw from university a month ago after the incident with her legs. No homework, no tests—it had been delightful for a moment, but all the TV and video games and books she wanted were not worth the price of bed sores and never again getting to pick flowers or lie in the grass or jump through autumn leaves. Never again getting to go out to dinner or to the beach with friends or family. Never getting to go to Oktoberfest where she could buy cupcakes the size of her face and funnel cake that left powder all over her clothes.

Now she was here, her life on hold, like a CD that was scratched and might not ever play again. But the worst part, for her, was knowing that her life was still incomplete. As tragic as a musician gone deaf in the middle of composing his concerto, a Michelangelo gone blind before David and La Pieta and the Sistine Chapel. How could she die without having ever done anything worthwhile? What a waste of a heart! Oh, all such a waste! If only she had known—maybe she wouldn't have wasted so much time hating and comparing and envying and judging and wishing and complaining. Maybe she would have spent just a little time loving and doing what she loved.

Now who was there for her to love? Who would choose a bird with a wounded wing when there were hundreds of clever parrots and strong eagles to be had instead?

The young girl turned her face away from the sun as a tear quietly rolled down her cheek. Who would ever fall in love with her now?

The sound of a leaf blower revving up drew her attention back to the window. It was just the gardener of their residential complex clearing away freshly-cut grass clippings outside. After a while, he saw her looking at him, turned off the blower, smiled and waved at her, and then set back to work.

He did that almost every day—smile. Come to think of it, he always looked so peaceful, so happy. Some days, when her window was open, she could hear him humming songs while he trimmed hedges and watered flowers. Where did that persistent, tenacious happiness come from, day in and day out?

Spurred by a sudden intense desire to know, she leaned over to grab the baby monitor from the bed. Papa hadn't worked in a while, so he stayed home with her during the day while Mama worked.

"Hey, Paps?" she said over the monitor, knowing he would hear.

A moment later, he entered her room, smiling. He always smiled when she called him Paps.

"What do you need, my bluebird?"

She gazed out the window at the gardener, who had become an abrupt subject of her attention.

"Can we invite him to dinner with us this evening?"

Papa raised an eyebrow, then shook his head with a grin. After so long he had gotten used to all the strange ideas his daughter got into her head.

"Sure," he said. "I'm sure he'd like that. In fact—" Papa dashed out of the room for a moment and then returned with her wheelchair. "Why don't you ask him yourself? It's about noon now; I'll wheel you out to the living room and tell him someone would like to talk to him on his lunch break."

The girl suddenly turned flustered, thinking she may have gotten too much in over her head.

"But I—my hair—I've lost so much weight—"

"You're beautiful," Papa said emphatically.

She sighed. "Now you're just trying to make me feel better."

He shook his head. "If he's a gardener worth his salt, then he will be able to see that your heart is full of roses."

A tender smile colored her cheeks like cherry blossoms dust the ground in early spring.

Still, she could not stop herself from wondering if—from hoping that—this gardener might know how to save dying roses. Of course, it was a lot of faith to hang on this man she didn't even know, but she was running out of places to hang it at all.

Papa lifted her out of bed and helped her to get dressed. It was a long time since she had worn anything other than pajamas, so she picked out one of her favorite outfits, a creamy yellow gingham dress and a little beige sunhat with a bow that Papa had given her a few years ago. "It just reminded me of you," he'd said when she asked what the occasion was. She put her dark, curly hair into a bun peeking out from under the side of the hat to try to hide the places where it was thinning.

Before she could even ask how she looked, Papa kissed her on the forehead and said, in a voice rich and deep as cacao, "You are lovely."

"Thou art all fair, my love, and there is no spot in thee," the girl murmured absentmindedly to herself as Papa's words drew her favorite song to mind.

Papa wheeled her out to the living room, right in front of the bay window she adored, and left her there for a moment while he went to get the gardener. As the two of them passed by the window, she heard much laughter, flowing like a running stream, like music. Her heart ached with nostalgia. There had not been such exuberant laughter in this house for a long time.

*Could I, even suffering, sorrowful me, sing with laughter, too?* she wondered.

When he entered behind Papa and saw her sitting there, he smiled at her. For the first time, she smiled back. It touched her—day in and day out, whether rain or shine, frost or heat—he always had a smile for her. He was like a bastion of happiness, goodness, beauty, and joy when so much around her and in her was patently not.

"Make yourself comfortable," Papa called from the kitchen as he started pulling out some lemons to make fresh lemonade for them.

The gardener sat in the sill of the bay window, not wanting to ruin their furniture since he had been working. The knees of his jeans were worn and caked in dirt and grass stains. He wore thick leather gloves that he pulled off before extending his hand to her. She noticed a scar on it as she gave him her hand.

He wrapped his other hand around hers for a moment as he said, "It is good to finally meet you."

She nodded, laughing nervously. "After seeing each other from afar through the window for so long, I am glad we can speak face to face."

As she leaned back into her wheelchair, folding her hands over her lap, he looked in her eyes, rather intently, and said, "Now that we are face to face, what do you want to say to me?"

His eyes were kind and gentle still, but serious now.

"Well, Papa and I wanted—"

There was a conspicuous cough from the kitchen.

The gardener grinned as though he knew something she did not.

Shaking her head a little bit, she began again, "I wanted to…"

She trailed off, staring fixedly out the window so that he would not be able to see the distress reflected in her face. What would he want with her, a sick little girl in a wheelchair? Why would he care at all, let alone take an interest in befriending her?

"I'm sorry for wasting your time," she said suddenly, giving him a polite smile. "I feel very silly."

"I do not think you are wasting my time at all," he replied firmly. "But if you would rather I go..." He stood up.

She watched him walk toward the door, her heart sinking with every step. She really wished to speak with him, this kind man, though she couldn't say why.

*This may be my last chance... Even if it's just a friendship out of pity, this may be my last chance... to love.*

"Stay!" she called after him, and oh, was she astonished that love could make a hawk out of a mouse!

He sat down in the bay window again, and it was not long before Papa brought out the lemonade. He went across the hall to the family room to watch his beloved westerns, leaving them to talk.

Before she could lose her nerve again, she said, "I wanted to invite you to dinner with us this evening."

"I would be delighted to," he said. "Just tell me...what made you think to ask me to dinner?"

"What do you mean?" she asked, avoiding the question.

"I'm the gardener," he replied. "People hardly notice me, let alone invite me into their home for dinner."

She smiled a little. "I don't know. There's just something about you, your joy."

"My joy?" he parroted, smiling playfully.

She laughed in spite of herself, covering her mouth with her hand as though trying to keep it in. "Yes, that right there!"

He became serious again. "Do you think joy is a secret?"

"A very well kept one," she said in a subdued voice. "For I've searched everywhere and still can't find it."

"And what makes you think that I have it? That is to say, if you have never experienced it, how would you recognize if you had found it?"

The young girl looked at his face. The skin around his eyes and the corners of his mouth were permanently stretched by crinkle lines. "I do not know what it looks like, but I think that it would look like what I see in you."

The young man's eyes positively danced. They flickered like the flame of a candle, undulating like waves of fire.

"Well," he said, standing as he slipped his gloves back on. "Perhaps I will be able to mark an X on the map to guide you to your treasure."

The circadian rhythm
teaches all creatures
that day follows closely
upon the heels of night.

But it can be tricked.
Bright light

in the dead of night
can pass for day.

A bird enfolded
in the pitch blackness
of a sheet
can mistake noonday
for midnight.

But what if one
were to open a window,
to take the bird
shrouded in darkness
out into the sun?

What if she were
to feel
the heat of the sun
upon her face?

What then?
Would she begin to realize
the darkness was
an illusion?

Mama was overjoyed when she returned home and heard that they were having company for dinner. The young girl had turned reclusive since becoming bedridden. In her sorrow and suffering, she cut herself off from everyone except her parents, and in some ways, even them. Therefore, when Mama heard that she had invited someone to dinner, she was pleasantly surprised.

Though being bedridden was a ponderous burden, it had been almost as unbearable for the young girl to go anywhere else in the house. Everything she saw reminded her of her old life before the illness: the bay window where she used to curl up in the late afternoon sun and read, the library where she used to entertain her friends and play video games on the TV with them, the kitchen where she would taste all Mama's food as she cooked, even the dining room where she had gotten her head stuck in one of the chairs. All those memories, all those things she could never do again. Or at least, that was what she had thought before today.

Sitting near the bay window, talking to that man, she realized that she could still do those things that she loved—that just because she could not do them the same way as before did not mean that she could not do them at all.

So she remained in the wheelchair, which she theretofore rarely used—only another reminder of her illness—and wheeled herself into the kitchen to help Mama cook. And by help Mama cook, she meant taste everything before it was done, which was, after all, exactly what she did before she lost the use of her legs.

She smiled as she snuck a spoon of peas into her mouth.

"And what are you grinning about?" Mama swatted her hand away as she went back for another taste.

"I was just thinking," the young girl mused, "I don't know how I could forget that you don't need legs to enjoy a good meal."

"You don't need legs to help peel those potatoes either."

She looked at Mama, mid-spoon to her mouth, and they both laughed so hard their sides hurt.

After another hour of clandestine taste-testing and helping to set the table, the doorbell rang just as the sun was setting and they were bringing out the serving platters.

"I'll get the door!"

When she opened the door, she hardly recognized who she saw there. A few hours ago, his dark brown hair had been pulled back from his face in a rough ponytail, and he had been wearing a white, short-sleeved t-shirt with a checkered jacket tied around his waist and faded jeans with mud and grass stains at the knees. Now, his dark, slightly wavy hair hung almost to his shoulders, his beard was trimmed, and he wore a dress shirt and some khaki pants. In his hand he held a bouquet of tulips.

He plucked a yellow tulip from the bouquet and held it out to her. Gesturing to her hair, he said softly, "May I?"

She had forgotten that she had taken off the hat when she was helping in the kitchen, and she'd never put it back on.

After a pause she nodded, and he bent down and wove the tulip through her hair. Before she could say anything, he whispered in a low voice, "Sorrow is not the enemy of joy."

She turned around to look at him as he pushed her wheelchair into the dining room. He merely smiled.

After all the pleasantries and introductions were exchanged, and the tulips were placed in a vase at the center of the table, dinner was served. There was lamb, spinach, yams, white beans, and macaroni.

"May I say the blessing?"

"We would be honored," Papa said.

They joined hands and bowed their heads as the gardener blessed the food.

"Thank you, Father, for this family, for the love that was put into this meal, for the love that moved them to open their home to me. Please heal this young woman through and through, and show her the true way to the joy she seeks. Amen."

She had scarcely picked up her fork when Papa exclaimed, "Oh, honey, I think 47 Ronin is on tonight!"

Mama sent one of her no-nonsense glares Papa's way. "*And?*"

"And I think we need to go watch it." Papa stared at her a long time and then winked.

Before she could even say, "What in the world," they had excused themselves and she was left alone at the table with the young man.

He tried valiantly to hide it, but she caught the trace of a smile quivering about his lips.

"You knew!" she said, waiting for him to meet her eyes.

He held up his hands in surrender. "Yes. When I was walking here with your father to meet you at lunch, he told me he had a little plan."

She shook her head, chuckling. "I should have known."

He caught her eye and said, "Your father is worried about you. That is why he wanted to give you the chance to talk with me alone."

The hair of a thinning eyebrow raised. "Why?"

"He told me that you have been distancing yourself from the people who love you, and he hoped that maybe you would decide to talk to me."

A slight shift of her face, the setting of her jaw like flint, betrayed the walls that were hastily going up brick by brick in her heart.

"If I won't even talk to my own family or friends about how I feel, then what makes you think I would talk to you?"

She regretted the words as soon as they were out of her mouth. "I'm sorry, I'm so very sorry." She closed her eyes and put her face in her hands.

The young girl jumped when she felt the warmth of his hand on hers across the table.

They sat in silence for minutes as she tried to rewind her thoughts that had exploded and unraveled like the tape in a VHS.

"Answer me this," he broke the silence gently yet strongly. "There was something that made you reach out to me, was there not?"

"Yeah." She could barely get the words out of her throat—it was a quiet admission, but it was enough.

"Look at me," he said suddenly.

She did.

"If you want to tell me anything, you needn't worry about anyone else knowing. After all," a grin began to bud on his face, "Plants don't have ears."

She laughed. She had been doing that a lot lately, since he had come into her life, and it had only been a day.

Perhaps the painful words that were stuck in her throat, that she hadn't been able to choke out with Mama in the middle of the night—perhaps they were now ready to come out.

She took a deep breath and began.

"I'm so confused. Despite all my symptoms, the doctors still have been unable to come up with a diagnosis. No diagnosis means no treatment, no prognosis, no... nothing. It's like walking in a dark tunnel to who knows where on a journey for who knows how long. Am I nearing the end, I wonder, or do I still have miles to go?"

She closed her eyes, fearing his reaction to what she was about to say. "I hope I am nearing the end."

Somehow, his eyes said more than his words ever could have. They were like pools, endless springs, of compassion and empathy.

"It is like I am Schrödinger's patient, both healthy and sick at the same time because I never know if I will get better, if I will recover completely or relapse permanently.

"No one understands how much I suffer." And there

it was, what she had been choking on for so long, for the whole year she had been sick. With that dislodged, everything else came coughing, retching up. "All my pain is invisible—I sometimes wonder if they even believe me. It is so easy to have pity on someone who is coughing up blood or waking with night sweats or covered in a rash or lying in a hospital bed, but I look perfectly normal on the outside.

"No one knows how horrifying it is to scratch your head and have hair come back on your hand, to breathe and then suddenly feel like a knife is tearing through your chest, to laugh and then be punched in the back, to have your arms and legs feel like they are turning to stone..."

She was sobbing all over her food, so hard that she could not stop, could hardly catch her breath.

"No one knows what it's like for your whole world to be turned upside down in an instant and yet have everyone around you go on acting as if nothing had happened at all and everything is the same!"

As she choked herself on her tears, the young man ran around the table and wrapped his arms around her, one hand rubbing and patting her back and the other holding her head. She was so little that her wails shook her whole frame.

After a while, she calmed down and pulled away from him to look up at his face. "What are you going to say to my pain? What words could you possibly offer in the face of so much suffering without them sounding hollow?"

Looking down into her eyes, he declared, "I see it. To your invisible pain, I say that I see it."

For whom
do you sing?

Some, shy,
would prefer
to sing alone,
unheard.

But for others,
a song sounds
less sweet
unless it is heard.

And birds?
Why do they
sing?

Why,
for one another—
to call to one another,
to communicate.

Songs are
for birds
what words are
for us.

## Becoming the Dawn

For a bird
to sing
she must have
someone in her heart
she is singing for.

Perhaps that is why
the bluebird
beneath the sheet
does not sing.

Not because she is mute,
or songless,
but because she is
loveless.

Yet one day,
somehow,
through the dark,
hidden in a place
where even the sun
could not reach her,
a cardinal came.

A cardinal
came to
the bluebird

and dwelled in the dark
with her.

Over the next two weeks, the young girl was in significantly more pain than normal, her condition likely exacerbated by the full brunt of her emotional state. Her parents tried to hide their worry, but she knew they were growing increasingly concerned, and this only saddened her all the more. She had asked to be moved to the couch in the living room during the day, and as she lay there, fearing her time might be slipping away, she continued to feel like something was missing, incomplete.

The gardener would come to visit her on his lunch breaks, and sometimes in the evenings as well, and one afternoon she asked him, "What can make life truly meaningful?"

He looked down at the palms of his hands, and her eyes followed his to the scars there, one on each of them. "Elaborate your question," he murmured, almost absentmindedly. She had never seen him behave quite like this before.

"All of the things that I used to do before I got sick seemed fulfilling at the time. The achievements and successes, the months' worth of hours of video games, the tireless effort I put into keeping up a spotless self-image that was at least as good as, hopefully better than, everyone else's."

She paused for a moment to focus on her breathing as her chest began to hurt again.

"But now here I am, facing the possibility, if not the imminent actuality, of an early death, and I feel unfulfilled. I have trophies and pins and certificates, the respect of my peers, yet something still feels lacking. If not those things, then what?"

"What indeed," he mused, still staring at the scars on his hands. Just as quickly as he had gone into his strange reticence, he emerged from it and said, "When you die, what do you hope to leave behind?"

The answer came to her lips unbidden. "A fragrance."

He looked at her, cocking an eyebrow.

"Just the way dried roses still retain the fragrance they had in life long after they are dead, so I would like to leave the fragrance of my heart behind me."

Smiling wistfully, he hummed, "That is perfectly lovely."

From her tired breast came forth a sigh. "But my heart is not so lovely as a rose in life and so cannot be in death. The garden of my heart has been decimated by anger and despair."

Here he smiled as brightly as she had ever seen. "Garden, you say? I have been known to have quite the green thumb."

And they both laughed. That was the end of the conversation that day, but he came back again on Saturday. It was the week before Easter, and so had warmed significantly so that she was able to go outside. She had taken to staying on the couch instead of the bed now, with her wheelchair by the bay window in case she needed to be moved, so when he arrived that morning she asked him to help her into the wheelchair.

"You won't be needing that today," he said.

"But I can't—"

"Walk? Yes, I know."

He scooped her up easily into his arms, and said, "I will be your legs today."

Her eyes were as wide and transparent as the bay window she adored when she glanced up at him. In her mind's eye, she suddenly saw the image of a bird with a bandaged wing being picked up and cupped in a pair of large hands. The hands belonged to an angel with the grandest pair of wings she had ever seen, and the angel took off into the matchless blue sky, still with the little bird cupped safely in its hands. *When you cannot fly, little bird, I will soar for you*, she heard.

She began to get a feeling that this young man was far more than just a mere gardener.

"Where are we going today?" she asked as they set out from her house. He walked slowly and gently so as not to jostle her too much, and she loved the way he would look down into her eyes to respond to her.

"The best place on earth to teach you to die meaningfully—a garden."

"Hey," she said after they had been walking in silence for a while. "How do you know so much about death and dying?"

He smiled cryptically. "I went to a garden once, a long time ago."

She was quite the little inquisitor today. "Do you think I will really die soon?"

He took a long time, a very long time, to respond—so long she began to doubt that he heard her. But he had. "It is never too soon to start preparing for death. It does not matter so much if you die sooner or later, so long as you are ready."

She exhaled a long breath and looked out at all the trees they were passing. They were lined up on either side of the quaint cobble path, forming a canopy of shade overhead that the sunlight stippled through. At last, when the path opened up to a clearing painted with yellow wildflowers, she knew they had arrived. There was one towering oak tree nestled toward the back, and the rest of the clearing was hedged in by bushes flowering in pinks and fuchsias and lavenders and violets.

As he was about to set her down in the grass she said, "You know, I've always wanted to climb a tree, but I was always afraid to."

His eyes crinkled and creased like a napkin, folding into the familiar shape of the smile she had come to cherish over the past weeks she had known him. "Then I will be your bravery as well." He lifted her onto his back, telling her to hold on tightly, and she giggled as he began to climb up into the enormous oak tree. They went about halfway up before they found a thick branch that they were able to comfortably rest on. Up there the breeze was generous, and the leaves hid them from the heat of the day. Down below, they could see the whole garden and all its variety of flowers spread out before them.

"This sight is more beautiful than anything I ever saw on my own two feet," she gasped.

He looked at her most lovingly, with a serene expression on his face. "X marks the spot." His voice was barely above a whisper. "The well-kept secret of joy, the thing that is needed to make life meaningful, the art of dying well—all those treasures are one and the same, and are buried right here."

She looked at the glorious beauty all around them. "Buried in this garden?"

He shook his head. "No. Buried in the words you just spoke."

"I don't understand."

"You said it yourself—you have found a vista more beautiful than anything you had ever seen when you were well.

"The secret to joy is that sorrow is not the thief of joy. The secret to a meaningful life is that death does not erase every trace of life. And the secret to dying well is knowing that, in some manner, you will live on."

"The secret to sickness, then…is—"

She began to cry as she discovered for herself the priceless buried treasure he had been leading her to. "The secret to sickness is that even in a sick body the heart can still be well."

He took her hand in his, gently brushing her palm with his thumb. "Yes. This is why I smile."

Weeping from joy, her heart said, *"And this will be why I sing."*

The cardinal
taught the bluebird
not how to sing,
but why.

For she did not need
a song,
she did not need
a voice,
she did not need
a rehearsal.
All she needed
was a reason.

And this
unlocked her heart,
freeing the
first notes
of her song
even while
still in the dark.

When the gardener carried her home later that evening, she was exuberant. Her tired body was radiant. She had never looked more beautiful.

After he left, Mama and Papa sat down on the couch with her and said, "What did you do today that has made you so happy, my little bird?"

She could not stop smiling. "I did not do anything," she said. "I saw everything."

She giggled at their confusion.

"Everything is the same as it was before," she continued, "but everything is different. I see it all differently. Do you remember when I got my glasses, and I said, 'Mama, Papa, the trees look so clear and sharp!' And Mama, you said, 'That is how they are supposed to look!' Well, it is just like that with my soul! Everything looks as it is supposed to now, as it was meant to be seen all along."

Mama and Papa's hands found each other and intertwined. There were tears in Mama's eyes.

"Maybe we need to get to know this gardener, too," Papa laughed.

Oh what joy, what fullness of joy in that house!

And it had not come a moment too soon. The very next day, she was in so much pain she sweated through the night and did not have the strength to let herself be moved from the bed that day. Mama and Papa sat on either side of her bed, looking at her with so much disappointment and worry.

"We had hoped that if your soul healed—" Mama began.

"Then your body would follow," Papa finished.

She looked at them very seriously. The radiance that had shone through her body yesterday was now hardly visible, but if you looked closely, you could find it hiding in her eyes. "I know it is hard to hear—it is just as hard to say—but if I die, do not be sad. I will not be gone forever. Like a bird I will leave behind a feather, so that even when I am gone, I will still remain with you.

"If I do get better, I honestly do not know what I shall do. I am so much happier now than when I was well. But if I have learned to find joy in sickness then surely I will now also be able to find it when I am well!"

She was so joyful that her parents could not help but smile, and that was all she could ask. She knew it was hard on them, and would be so much harder after she was gone. That was why she wanted them to smile and laugh as much as they could now, so that they could remember her and, in so doing, remember to smile again. Even when she was gone.

The days passed and it looked like she would not get well after all. Her hair, which had been coming out for the past two months, was now almost all gone. Where once the pain had come and gone infrequently, leaving periods of seemingly normal health, now the pain was constant. She was nauseous often and could not keep down food well. In a few days it was evident that she was far gone, and despite all the in-home doctor visits, samples run back and forth between the lab, still they did not know what was wrong or what to do. That word which many see as a curse or death sentence—palliative care—was uttered.

The gardener came daily, but was unable to see her for long because of her waning strength. She had only one thing left she wanted to say to him whom her soul loved.

"Thank you."

He smiled, leaned over her, and kissed her on the forehead.

Mama and Papa spent every minute by her bedside, and so did that little bunny she had carried around since second grade—Quincy.

"I feel like him," she joked in between breaths. "Patched up over and over again."

The young girl leaned her tired head against her mother's chest, finally now happy and at peace.

"Mama, Papa, remember," she said, turning to look at them for the last time. "The secret is that silence cannot hush the bluebird's song. The priceless treasure that my dear friend has given to me I will give to you: suffering is not the thief of joy. And no matter how deep the darkness gets, it can never truly erase the light."

The black sheet,
the dreaded veil
obscuring the sun
which had never
stopped shining—
the veil was
torn in two.

Light flooded
the lightless place.

The bluebird
whose heart
had been opened
to sing
opened the bars
of the cage.

The cardinal
waiting for
the bluebird
to sing
now bellowed
his noble song.

The red bird
and the blue bird,
they sang together.

Wings flapped,
stirred up a breeze
as they both
flew forth from the cage.

The bluebird

shed a feather
as she soared.

It floated down
to the earth—
a promise that
all who were caged
could fly—

That was
the bluebird's song.

## After years of

sitting in the dark,

waiting
for the sun to rise
for me,

to bestow its light
and joy
and warmth
on me
the way it has
on so many others,

I became impatient.
I decided
to stop waiting
for the sun
to rise
in my life.

I decided
to become the dawn
for myself.

## Acknowledgements

Thank you to my mom for always being my light. You are my role model for a life well lived, because from watching you every day I learned that just because life is hard does not mean it can't also be happy and full of laughter and smiles. I would not be here without you.

Thank you to my dad for always nagging me with the question, "When are you going to publish your writing?" When I told you I was going to make my own website to post my poems, you said there were people who needed my words and wouldn't be able to find them that way. You told me there were people that needed my book. Turns out you were right, and perhaps I am the person who needed this book the most.

Thank you, Sabrina, for being proud of me before I was proud of myself, and for telling me that I am awesome when sometimes I feel like I'm not anything special.

Thank you, Michael, for giving me the idea to read my poems at our local poetry night. And for reading all the poems I sent you screenshots of over Instagram, even though there were a lot.

Thank you, Lisa and Taleasha, for being my cheerleaders for this book and for wishing it to be everything I've dreamed of.

Thank you, Miranda, for helping me believe that my dreams are possible. I never would have been brave enough to publish this book without you.

Thank you to Shelby Leigh for helping this book reach its fullest potential and to reach all the people it was meant to.

Thank you to Islam Farid for giving me a more beautiful cover than I could have ever imagined and helping this book feel alive.

Thank you to my readers for buying this book and making my dream of touching people's lives with my books come true.

## About the Author

Jay W. Song is a full-time pharmacist who has a heart for helping people heal, whether through medicine or through stories. She writes her books hoping that they will make others feel seen, and that they will inspire others to discover the unique joy their life can bring, even in difficult circumstances. When she isn't helping patients or working on her next book, you can find her hoarding new books like a dragon, yelling at her Nintendo Switch, or picking flowers.

Keep up with her on Instagram **@authorjaywsong** or on her website **jaywsong.co**

www.ingramcontent.com/pod-product-compliance
Lightning Source LLC
Chambersburg PA
CBHW020332010526
44119CB00002B/36